Experiential Psychotherapy with Children

**The Johns Hopkins Series in
Contemporary Medicine and Public Health**

Consulting editors:

Samuel H. Boyer IV, M.D.
Gareth M. Green, M.D., M.P.H.
Richard T. Johnson, M.D.
Paul R. McHugh, M.D.
Edmond A. Murphy, M.D.
Albert H. Owens, Jr., M.D.
Edyth H. Schoenrich, M.D., M.P.H.
Jerry L. Spivak, M.D.
Barbara H. Starfield, M.D., M.P.H.

Also of interest in the series:

The Perspectives of Psychiatry
Paul R. McHugh, M.D., and Phillip R. Slavney, M.D.

Practical Comprehensive Care of Anorexia and Bulimia
Arnold E. Andersen, M.D.

*Family Management of Schizophrenia: A Study of Clinical, Family,
and Economic Benefits*
Ian R. H. Falloon, M.D., and Others

Neuropsychological Rehabilitation after Brain Injury
George P. Prigatano and Others

Experiential Psychotherapy with Children

Logan Wright, Frances Everett,
and Lois Roisman

THE JOHNS HOPKINS UNIVERSITY PRESS
Baltimore and London

The Johns Hopkins University Press,
701 West 40th Street,
Baltimore, Maryland, 21211
The Johns Hopkins Press Ltd., London

The paper in this book is acid-free and meets the guidelines for permanence and durability of the Committee on Production Guidelines for Book Longevity of the Council on Library Resources.

Library of Congress Cataloging-in-Publication Data
Wright, Logan, 1933–
  Experiential psychotherapy with children.

  (The Johns Hopkins series in contemporary medicine and public health)
  Bibliography: p.
  Includes index.
  1. Experiential psychotherapy for children. I. Everett, Frances. II. Roisman, Lois. III. Title. IV Series. [DNLM: 1. Psychotherapy—in infancy & childhood.   WS 350.2 W951e]
RJ505.E87W75 1986   618.92′8914   85-23915
ISBN 0-8018-3298-5 (alk. paper)

Contents

Foreword

Children are special—in them the perfection of nature is so obvious. What causes the child to grow, from seed and infancy, into one elaborate stage after another? Not the child's own planning, surely, nor ours. That inwardly arising developmental process, if it is not utterly obstructed, moves in its own endlessly complex way. It has made us all and goes on in every child before our eyes.

With children it does not strain our adult beliefs to trust the inwardly arising process, because that is the obvious part. We worry about our child-rearing practices, of course, but we know them to be a small part, an opening for us to add something. Most of our concern should be about not getting in the way of growth and development.

Client-centered therapy is based on the fact that living organisms are the result of an inwardly originating growth process, and that wounds and difficulties also heal by a natural process. We cleanse wounds or sew stitches, and that helps, but the healing comes from inside.

Client-centered therapists give their attention, caring, and exact understanding to each and every bit of expression of the client. To understand means to check out loud: "They hurt your feelings when they said you came in last, is that right?" Usually the client has a correction, then, "No, I did come in last, and that's okay; since I did, it was true. But they didn't have to say it. They said it to put me down." "Oh," says the therapist, "it hurt that they put you down and that they wanted to put you down." "Yes" (silence). There is usually a sigh of relief, when the message is understood just as it was intended. A peace comes inside. That much has gotten across. There is a space inside. Something new can then come from inside to fill that space.

Therapists who have never consistently checked their understanding in this way do not know how far they often are from understanding the other person. Only the actual checking would reveal how often they miss.

Early in life we give up expecting to be understood completely. Other people seldom want to know exactly how anything is for us, how we are living, sensing, and meaning. Most of us are glad if others are not too violently insulting or utterly impervious, and if their judgments are at least friendly or well-intentioned.

Carl Rogers discovered that if every bit of a client's self-expression is taken in by the therapist, checked, verified, and then left to stand as is, without editing, without adding, without "correcting" and "improving" and "interpreting," then this inner relief and space lets more and more come from inside until a self-propelled change process rises in the client. Adding a combination of other techniques can help at times, but too much interference prevents the powerful process from getting started. Then there are only the pot shots and efforts of the therapist and the deliberate efforts of the client, which add up to very little in comparison.

Client-centered therapy was discovered with children: Rogers began his work with children, and his work comes from the earlier work of J. Taft and F H. Allen. So the use of client-centered therapy with children is not an "application" to children—Rogers used it with them for some time before he tried it with adults.

It is characteristic of the inwardly arising steps of this process that what at first seems irrational and negative opens up into "Oh, of course, that makes sense. Of course, I don't eat lunch when I'm anxious. Of course, I'm anxious if I think my mother prefers my little brother. Of course, it makes a sinking feeling in my stomach when I think of leaving them home alone together." At first the child might have said, "I don't eat lunch because I'm not hungry." This would have been true, yet the statement would have had a fuzzy edge, a hint of something more. When people are fully heard without argument or addition, the peace that then comes allows them to sense the remainder, the "more." Typically, though not as quickly as in my example, steps of opening up come about. The "more" opens into whatever comes, and that in turn leaves its edge, its "more," till that, too, opens into another step.

Experiential therapy is a further development, especially appropriate for people who do not experience this gradual opening up, even after some time. The aim of experiential therapy is exactly the same as that of client-centered therapy—to engender this inwardly arising process. What can a therapist do when the client offers nothing or very little to respond to? How can a therapist sense, attend to, be with, these "edges," this "more," if the client does not attend to them?

Obviously, interpreting or guessing what might come from these edges would skip the actual, physically felt steps, and so would only "tell" the client some outside opinions. Even if one guesses something like that out loud, the helpful part is not the correctness but the invitation to the person to attend, to sense, to experience the actual inward opening. Therefore, making guesses or interpretations about these edges tentative does more than indicate an accepting attitude. Rather, this tentativeness is an invitation to the client to sense directly, and thereby perhaps to get a concrete, organismic step of inward movement. More recently, psychotherapists have also developed direct ways of talking about this edge even while it is as yet unclear, in order to help a person focus on it.

Children often give a therapist nothing verbal about themselves at first. They do not share the adult's nearly exclusive concern with words, or rather, pretended concern with words. Adults are trained socially to proceed smoothly with conversation even when all the concrete living signs belie the words. Adult clients can continue for a long time on mere social politeness. Fortunately, many children cannot, though this makes problems for the exclusively verbal therapist.

How do therapists come to understand children? How do they intepret nonverbal play? What about the child who does not wish to come to therapy or does not want to enter the therapy room? This book considers these and other issues. Experiential therapy turns difficulties in relating to children into opportunities to get deeper responses.

If therapists are not to judge and impose interpretations, where can they find responses? In two places, in the direct experiences of themselves and of their clients. But therapists must not dump feelings and reactions on the child. When is self-expression such dumping and when and how is it a sensitive response? What are the criteria for determining what to say?

Moving beyond client-centered reflection is not a compromise between different goals. Rather, a flexible approach serves to further the same goal, which is the inwardly arising process itself. The therapist decides what to say by asking, "Will whatever I intend to say or do help the inward sensing, make the safety and space for it, or will it crowd, impose, distract from the child's own track?"

This book is full of lovely detail about how to work closely with a child without imposing or distracting. It deals with just those specifics therapists want help with: when touching helps intimacy, when to put a hand on a child's shoulder, how to avoid phoniness. Direct talk is good, but belittling the child's concerns cannot help. When should the therapist say, "I have feelings like that, too. Everyone does"? How can one really convey that one wants to understand and be close, yet still respect the child's right not to be intimate in return?

Some of the examples are so telling that three sentences can convey a whole principle of this practice. Here is a therapist working with an angry little girl who only looks out the window.

> *Therapist:* I wish you'd communicate with me directly, even just to say you're angry.
> *Child:* [*No response*]
> *Therapist:* And I'm not going to give up. I'm going to stick with you until you're over your problem. I care too much to give up, even when you seem to be telling me that you'd like for both of us to give up.

In this example the therapist expresses a helpful attitude without invading the child's rights. The example also shows the difference between actively "probing" and unobstrusively attending to the "edge." Experiential therapists accept *any* sort of expression from the child, however far from therapeutic matters. But they do not slip into a shallow, buddylike conversation. Instead, they remain clear-sighted, talking about affect but gladly receiving anything the child says.

In the early sessions the therapist does not express opinions about morals or decisions. When the child has long experienced the implicit self-determining in this therapy, then the therapist's values or views become only one datum, which can be weighted with much else. Only then can a therapist express opinions. There are many such distinctions.

This book is also of value to parents. Parents are not necessarily blamed for a child's problems. In line with the author's more sensitive understanding of the child, they show that a human being's difficulties are not "caused" in some one way. The authors give suggestions for specifically structured home play sessions that encourage the child to express feelings and issues that might otherwise be inappropriate. Such sessions are likely to be of great value.

I am happy to welcome this book. It is for professional psychotherapists most of all, but also for parents and anyone who is interested in human beings. Although it deals with hard issues, it does not lack sensitivity.

Eugene T. Gendlin

Acknowledgments

We would like to acknowledge the assistance of dedicated co-workers Karen Coleman, Jaye C. May, Jill Mizel, and Geri Price. We also give our very special appreciation to Shelly Craig for aid in library research essential to the preparation of this text.

Introduction

Helping Children
with Psychological Problems

Most children experience psychological problems at one time or another, and many have transient periods of mild emotional disturbance or behavioral difficulty. Indeed, the normal child is certainly not free of problems. Developmental reviews of "normal" children typically report a high prevalence of mild emotional and behavioral problems, such as oversensitivity, fearfulness, shyness, overactivity, disturbing dreams, or aggressiveness (Lapouse and Monk 1958, 1964; MacFarlane, Allen, and Honzik 1954; Werry and Quay 1971). Many of these problems dissipate with development and the passage of time. The natural resiliency of children enables many of them to cope with or overcome these problems and to progress and develop along healthy lines.

For some, however, the problems of childhood are not transient and are severe enough to interfere with healthy development and growth. For them, childhood is not a positive experience. These are the children who warrant professional attention, and it is for them that this book is written.

This book will focus on experiential therapy as one way of helping children, but we understand, and want you to understand, that experiential therapy is only one way of helping children. The appropriate approach must be decided upon after careful evaluation of all the factors affecting the child, internally and externally.

Helping the Child Directly

Psychotherapy provided directly to the child is indicated when the child's psychological problem is severe or when the involved adults (parents, guardians, teachers, etc.) are unwilling or unavailable to work on the problem. The therapy may take the form of a supportive/relationship approach, uncovering or dynamic psychotherapy, or behavior modification.

Supportive/Relationship Psychotherapy

The basic theoretical position of supportive/relationship therapy is that individuals have inherent self-actualizing potential, and this therapeutic approach fosters the process of self-actualization by promoting self-reliance, competency, and, by implication, self-esteem. Competency and self-esteem are important components of emotional development. Experiential psychotherapy is the most recently evolved form of supportive/relationship treatment.

Carl Rogers has been a primary source of light in the area of supportive/relationship psychotherapy. The chapters that follow describe applications of recent Rogerian-type thinking to work with children. No theorist has been more willing than Rogers to subject his ideas to empirical scrutiny and to modify his methods in accordance with the results. Consequently, that which constitutes *the* Rogerian approach must continually be revised and restarted. And this process as it applies to children has lagged far behind the application to adults. Our purpose in this text is to close that gap. We have tried to keep the text simple and straightforward, digestible by all who work with children.

Volumes of data have accumulated on the evolution of Rogerian psychotherapy, although the approaches described are sometimes referred to by different names (e.g., client-centered, experiential, existential/phenomenologic, etc.). Most works have been concerned with applying these theories to adults; we believe that therapists and students need a text that relates these findings to children. Virginia Axline, Elaine Dorfman, and Clark W. Moustakas have all contributed in this regard, but no one has yet applied to children the insights gained by Rogers and his colleagues in recent years and since their experiences in working with psychotic patients. Eugene Gendlin, a colleague of Rogers, has developed from those encounters with schizophrenic clients an approach known as experiential therapy, and it is from that branch of the Rogerian tree that we grow.

Having noted that the Rogerian style is to remain open to change, we are constrained by alterations that are occurring in the mental health care delivery system to examine where this therapy fits best and under what circumstances it may have less applicability. In his classic 1957 work, Rogers wrote of the "necessary *and* sufficient conditions of therapeutic personality change" (p. 95).

Since Rogers's theoretical and research work, as well as his own personal style, have always been characterized by objectivity, we assume that he would agree that certain emerging approaches to mental health care require more than we can provide through the experiential psychotherapeutic experiences described in this text. In other words, while a number of newer mental health care approaches might benefit from good experiential conditions, they may also go beyond them in ways that clearly help the client. Thus, there are occasions when experiential therapeutic approaches may be necessary but not sufficient.

Examples of such circumstances include the brief contacts that characterize "primary mental health care." Most of this care is delivered in pediatric, internal medicine, and family medicine settings. It usually involves medication or direct advice (Wright 1982). Since there are more mental health contacts in primary care settings (American Academy of Pediatrics 1978) than in mental health settings, brief consultations (usually five to fifteen minutes long) have become the modal form of mental health care in the United States (Wright 1982). Even with brief consultations, however, therapist congruence, sympathetic listening, valuing, the resulting relationship, and even keeping the locus of responsibility in perspective are necessary; all of these can facilitate treatment. The point is that with only five to fifteen minutes available on a once- or twice-a-year basis, medication, advice, bibliotherapy, and so on, may be indicated. Thus good conditions, while necessary, cannot be regarded as sufficient.

Uncovering or Dynamic Psychotherapy

Uncovering psychotherapy is sometimes called dynamic or psychoanalytically oriented psychotherapy. Regarding children, the classic works in this area are those by Melanie Klein (1932) and Anna Freud (1926, 1965). Klein was more orthodox in her application of this form of therapy; Freud presented what could be called a neo-Freudian approach for children, paralleling the work with adults of Harry Stack Sullivan (1953) and Karen Horney (1939).

Dynamic approaches to working with children typically assume that psychopathology has roots in early childhood. The dynamically oriented therapist tries to work through internalized conflicts and the transference neurosis using interpretation to bring unconscious material into awareness. Treatment is geared to (or varies with) the child's developmental level. Dynamically oriented therapists have been particularly concerned with children's developmental differences as they influence motivation for treatment, the capacity to form a transference neurosis, and the ability to free-associate.

Behavioral psychotherapy applies principles from experimental psychology to alleviate problems and promote more effective functioning. Behavior therapists assume that most behaviors are learned and that the most effective way to correct problems with behavior is through conditioning or learning techniques. On this basis, behavior therapists stress the "here and now," as opposed to early life events. They attempt to produce changes in overt behavior and assume that this will have an impact on thoughts and feelings.

Conditioning or behavior-modification techniques tend to be quite precise, and they are usually targeted at one highly specific behavior that is altered by carefully arranged techniques. Phobias and other neurotic symptoms are especially responsive to behavior modification (Wolpe 1969). These techniques are often the treatment of choice when a symptom threatens to exert a lasting effect on the child's development, as in the case of medical/psychological problems such as encopresis and self-induced seizures or life-threatening behaviors such as psychogenic vomiting or refusal to take medication.

Helping the Child Indirectly

Indirect techniques for helping children involve assisting those who participate in the rearing of the child to improve the quality of their own helping skills. This may entail consulting parents, allowing them to monitor their child's therapy, or training them as paraprofessional psychotherapists. Carkhuff and Bierman (1970), for example, gave parents group training in Rogerian interpersonal skills and obtained significant parental improvement on quantifiable measures of communication and adjustment. Wright (1976) reported a technique for indirectly treating mildly disturbed children by presenting principles of behavior to parents via a printed manual and structured group discussions. This method attempted to improve parental skill and understanding by teaching principles of behavior drawn from learning theory, self-concept theory, and psychoanalysis. The principles offered guidelines for relating to children in a variety of situations at different stages of development. Results of testing the parents before and after group discussions suggested that such consultation produces a significant impact on both the participants and their children. Such indirect treatment is thus deemed useful in that the professional's time is used economically and because it is a valid way to change parental attitudes and children's behavior.

Preventing Psychological Problems in Children

Community psychology has stressed the role of the environment in the development of the individual's adjustment difficulties. Community psychologists thus function as active intervenors manipulating environmental forces to alleviate human problems. An emphasis is placed on prevention. Such an emphasis, it is hoped, spares children and families needless suffering and minimizes the need for direct services.

Numerous potential preventive measures and programs have been developed for working with children and families. Caplan (1964) suggested distinguishing among prevention efforts in terms of their temporal focus. Primary prevention programs are designed to reduce the incidence of new cases of various types of disorders. Examples of these efforts could include such activities as providing preventive education for parents, teachers, and others who work with children, designing physically healthy environments for children (neighborhoods, day care centers, etc.), and designing appropriate play materials or toys. Secondary prevention efforts are aimed at reducing the duration or severity of a problem and might include early screening and early identification activities as well as early intervention or direct services for more moderate problems. Tertiary prevention consists of treatment of current difficulties and attempts to reduce long-term disability. At this level, direct services are usually required. Such distinctions illustrate the variety of broadly based community prevention programs that may be of benefit to children and their families.

An Outline for This Text

Being an effective therapist with children is subtle, difficult work, requiring full concentration. We have tried to communicate the difficulties and frustrations encountered as well as the rewards that can realistically be expected by client and therapist alike. In so doing, we single out five therapeutic conditions, but we recognize that this is an artificial fragmentation. In an orientation to therapy where *process* is the focus rather than content or technique, these conditions cannot be separated but must be blended together by the therapist. They are each manifestations of an attitude, a philosophy. Above all, the qualities of the therapist will determine whether a child undergoes constructive personality change.

After considering the historic roots of experiential psychotherapy, we will look at the partners in the immediate therapeutic experience: the therapist and the child. We will describe five therapeutic conditions (intimacy, congruence, valuing, empathy, and responsibility) that compose the psychological or inter-personal environment. Then we will discuss certain factors outside the therapist-client relationship itself which may influence it: the reactions of parents and others, the physical environment in which therapy occurs, and the importance of the beginning and ending sessions. To conclude, we will look at the outcome of the therapy.

I

The Evolution of Experiential Psychotherapy

> It is hypothesized that man, like every other living organism, plant or animal, has an inherent tendency to develop all his capacities in ways that serve to maintain or enhance the organism. This is a reliable tendency, which, when free to operate, moves the individual toward what is termed growth, maturity, life enrichment.
>
> —Rogers, *Client-centered Psychotherapy*

Carl Rogers's description of the tendency of humans to move toward self-actualization also depicts the process in which client-centered therapy has been engaged over the past four decades. From Roger's first thoughts about what constitutes effective therapy, the concept has evolved by stages over the years, benefiting from the research and insights of many participants.

When Rogers first voiced his theories, he was somewhat surprised to find that they were regarded as new. He believed that he was developing a way of working with individuals that drew from Sigmund Freud, Rank, and the mainstream of personality theory. Rogers was influenced as well by the work of E H. Allen concerning psychotherapy with children. Nonetheless, the uproar caused by his talk, "Newer Concepts in Psychotherapy," at the University of Minnesota in 1940 forced him to realize that his thought was not a branch on the Rankian tree, but indeed a new hybrid especially suited to the American environment and destined to extend in as yet unimagined directions. As "a way of being with people," his concepts, like those of Freud before him, have changed America's personality. Rooted firmly in phenomenology, Rogerian theory has altered American life outside the therapist's office, in industry, education, religion, politics, and family life.

Phenomenology

Most practitioners of supportive/relationship therapy maintain a phenomenologic rather than an empirical perspective of reality. Phenomenology is based on the belief that reality is different for each perceiver, whereas empiricism holds that there is only one reality. To the empiricist, the reality of the oak tree is within the tree. To the phenomenologist, each perceiver has his or her own vantage point from which the tree is seen, and each perception is real to that person; no two perceivers view the tree from precisely the same vantage point. If the tree falls, the empiricist believes there is sound. According to the phenomenologist, a psychotherapy client's view of reality is valid for the client even though the therapist's perception of the same reality may differ. There is no point, then, in discussing who is right or wrong in perceptions of reality; there is only the client's reality or the therapist's reality.

The Evolution of Rogerian Therapy

The phenomenological role was new for the therapist in the 1940s. In the early stage of what was then called nondirective therapy, the therapist set out to create a nonauthoritarian, permissive environment in which the client could be free to achieve insight into self and situation; the therapist's main role was to help the client clarify feelings and perceptions. In 1942, Rogers explained it this way:

> Effective counseling consists of a definitely structured, permissive relationship which allows the client to gain an understanding of himself to a degree which enables him to take positive steps in the light of his new orientation. This hypothesis has a natural corollary, that the techniques used should aim toward developing this free and permissive relationship, this understanding of self in the counseling and other relationships and this tendency towards positive self-initiated action. (p. 18)

During this period, the theories of client-centered therapy, as it had come to be called, were applied to children by Virginia Axline. Therapists using this method created a permissive environment where the child was free to behave as he or she chose, without defensiveness or fear of judgment or punishment.

> Nondirective play therapy may be described as an opportunity that is offered to the child to experience growth under the most favorable conditions. Since play is his

natural medium for self-expression, the child is given the opportunity to play out his accumulated feelings of tension, frustration, insecurity, aggression, fear, bewilderment, confusion. By playing out these feelings he brings them to the surface, gets them out in the open, faces them, learns to control them, or abandon them. When he has achieved emotional relaxation, he begins to realize the power within himself to be an individual in his own right, to think for himself, to make his own decisions, to become psychologically more mature, and by doing so, to realize selfhood. (Axline 1947, 16)

Research and accumulation of experience with supportive/relationship psychotherapy led over the years to modifications in the role of the therapist. For instance, the therapist was found to be more effective if he or she responded with sensitivity to the *felt* meaning rather than to the words of the client. Emphasis moved from the verbal content of the therapy sessions to their emotional content. Raskin (1951) described this more intense and focused response of the therapist.

Counselor participation becomes an active experiencing with the client of the feelings to which he gives expression. The counselor makes maximum effort to get under the skin of the person with whom he is communicating, he tries to get *within* and to live the attitudes expressed instead of observing them, to catch every nuance of their changing nature; in a word, to absorb himself completely in the attitude of the client. And in struggling to do this, there is simply no room for any other counselor activity or attitude; if he is attempting to live the attitudes of the other he cannot be diagnosing them, he cannot be thinking of making the process go faster. Because he is another, and not the client, the understanding is not spontaneous but must be acquired, and this through the most intense, continuous, and active attention to the feelings of the other, to the exclusion of other types of attention. (p. 29)

The next stage in the evolution of supportive/relationship therapy was marked by the experiences of Rogers and his co-workers in Wisconsin. It was there that the first concentrated efforts were made to use client-centered therapy with psychotic clients. Critics complained that it worked well enough with the students and faculty at the University of Chicago (where Rogers had been based), most of whom were highly intelligent, well-motivated, verbal, and psychologically minded people, but that it might not work with difficult clients. Such criticism spurred Rogers to try his theories with the severely disturbed.

The frustrations Rogers encountered working with nonverbal, passive, unmotivated schizophrenics led him to new insights into the therapeutic relationship. In particular, he developed a deeper appreciation of the role of congruence in therapy. Overtly, therapists were being sympathetic, calm, and patient, but inside they were frustrated, sometimes angry, and on occasion ready to give up. Long silences led therapists to begin to express their own emotions and to use these expressions as the material with which they dealt in therapy. Thus, they began to model the behavior (congruence—see chapter 3 for a detailed explanation of this term) they hoped to see in their clients.

In "The Necessary and Sufficient Conditions of Therapeutic Personality Change" (1957), Rogers set forth the idea that positive change would occur in a client when the therapist was empathic, held the client in positive regard, and was congruent with that client. By the late 1950s, as a result of the experience with psychotic clients, Rogers and his colleagues had come to consider congruence the key to any therapeutic relationship. This was a major change. Now it was understood that the therapist's transparency would serve the client. The therapist's feelings at the moment of therapy were available as data to the client; they were feedback as to how another person was responding to that client's behavior. Thus, the therapist could become a model for behavior as well as a giver of important information in order to help the client remove barriers to growth.

Emphasis was placed on the client's experiencing, and expression of the therapist's own experiencing often became an important part of the process. J. Seeman described this new function of the therapist.

> These emergent descriptions of the counselor's function had come to view the counselor as a more totally caring and participating person. These views served as a vital reservoir when client-centered therapists began to work with hospitalized psychotic persons. In this new setting, the patterns of verbal interaction which had worked in the community counseling center were not enough. The counselor had to reach the patient in other ways. The resources for such communication were found precisely in the developing attitudes of caring and participation. The patient might not be ready to involve himself in a relationship, but the therapist could. Even if the patient could not communicate himself, the therapist could. And though the patient could not offer his experience as a basis for contact, the therapist could. (1965, 1220–21)

By the late 1960s, the original Rogerian approach had evolved so far (Rogers himself had become a neo-Rogerian) that, in verbatim accounts of therapy, phenomenologic therapists could not be distinguished from those of other schools. This was in great contrast to the reflections of verbal content that had previously given away their orientation. The table displays the various stages in the evolution of Rogerian therapy.

Appropriate Uses of Different Psychotherapeutic Techniques

In the 1980s, any technique that serves the client's growth is an acceptable tool in supportive/relationship therapy. The therapist's reaction to transference was

Table

Periods in the Development of
Rogerian Psychotherapy

Time Frame	Functions of the Therapist	Personality Changes
Period I Nondirective Psychotherapy 1940–1950	Creation of a permissive, noninterventive atmosphere; acceptance and clarification.	Gradual achievement of insight into one's self and one's situation.
Period II Reflective Psychotherapy 1950–1957	Reflection of feelings; avoidance of threat in the relationship.	Development of congruence of self-concept and the phenomenological field.
Period III Experiential Psychotherapy 1957–	Use of a wide range of behaviors to express basic attitudes; focus on the client's experiencing; expression of the therapist's experiencing.	Growth in the continuing process of inter- and intrapersonal living promoted by learning to use direct experiencing.

previously considered a Freudian technique inappropriate to supportive/relationship therapy. Now it is seen as another form of therapist congruence which can provide new data. Eugene Gendlin (1974, 1981, 1986) summarized the evolution: "The basic principle we see more clearly today is: the client-centered response, which I now call *the experiential response,* is the honest untrammeled pointing at the client's *felt meaning.*" He went on to predict that there would be "a universal *experiential* method of psychotherapy using all useful procedures in reference to the individual's own process" (1974, 550). Indeed, such seems to be the trend, not only in individual psychotherapy but also in group process and other important relationships such as marriage and the family.

An eclectic therapist using psychotherapy as a helping tool will generally use either an uncovering approach or supportive/relationship therapy. If the therapist is dealing with adults, there are certain criteria for deciding which approach to use. If the client is extremely disturbed and perhaps on the verge of personality decompensation or a psychotic break, an uncovering approach could provide untoward risk, stripping away rationalizations, denial, repression, and other defenses that may be useful in avoiding more severe forms of psychopathology. If, however, the person is not in any great danger of decompensation, these defenses can interfere with emotional growth. If nothing else, they stand as barriers between "normal" (i.e., average) adjustment and conspicuously adaptive behavior.

While there may be argument about the best form of therapy for adults, when children are the clients their nonverbal nature and their lack of sophisticated abstract thinking contraindicate dynamic or uncovering psychotherapy as we know its use with adults. To whatever degree one might believe that experiential therapy is appropriate for adults, it is many times more applicable for work with children.

2

Partners in Therapy

> In the development of client-centered psycho-
> therapy, there has gradually evolved the concept
> that therapeutic success is dependent not primarily
> on the technical training or skills of the therapist,
> but on the presence of certain attitudes in the
> therapist. When they are effectively communi-
> cated to and perceived by the client, these
> attitudes are considered to be the crucial determi-
> nants of therapeutic progress and
> constructive changes in personality.
>
> —Rogers, *Client-centered Psychotherapy*

Defining Therapy

Just as a worker must define the work to be done before choosing the proper tool, so must therapy be defined before describing the therapist. As the tool must fit the work, so the therapist must fit the therapeutic goals, for he or she is, indeed, the only tool. The carpenter has a saw, the mechanic has a wrench, but the psychotherapist has only himself or herself to refine, sharpen, and adjust to the job at hand.

An older, and for the most part discarded, conception was that therapy is a means of solving the client's problems; the therapist supposedly knows best and is in charge. The client generally completes such therapy with one problem only temporarily solved. Crisis intervention—short-term counseling where the client primarily lacks information (i.e., vocational-educational counseling)—may still be an appropriate vehicle for this model. Also, in the emerging area of medical psychology, in which the treatment of a symptom that threatens the development or even the life of the client requires that the therapist remove the symptom, it may be appropriate for the therapist to solve the client's problem.

A second definition of therapy is that it is a method of helping the client solve his or her own problems, moving the locus of responsibility from therapist to client. Adult clients often come to therapy with one pressing problem, and stop coming when that problem is solved. The difficulty with such a model is that the client has solved only one problem and may not be better equipped to cope with future challenges; indeed, many people use therapy as a means of solving problems, returning to the therapist whenever a new crisis arises.

The third and preferred definition, then, is that therapy is a way of helping the client to improve his or her problem-solving potential. The difference between this therapeutic model and the others is akin to the difference between helping a child pick out "Chopsticks" on the piano and teaching him or her to read music. The client leaves the therapy experience having learned a new set of skills which can be applied to all life problems. Such therapy can be used without ever discussing a particular problem. The process can focus on feelings rather than subject matter, on felt experience rather than verbal content. If a boy experiences a therapeutic relationship that enhances his ability to solve problems, then the therapist has successfully created an atmosphere where growth can occur. This is why supportive/relationship therapy is so effective with children; even though the boy may not be talking about his main problem as defined by others, he is experiencing a relationship in which he can grow and develop coping skills.

The fact that the "problem" is not being discussed does not mean that therapy is not occurring or that the proper form of therapy is not being conducted. In experiential therapy with children the emphasis is placed on what is happening at the moment between the therapist and the child in order to enhance the child's awareness of felt experience and to alter the quality of that experience. This change in the quality of experience generally results in greater self-esteem at the cognitive level and in more positive rather than negative emotion at the affective level. The therapist is constantly focusing on the immediate experience. This is quite different from uncovering, or insight-oriented, psychotherapy, which employs a kind of psychic archaeology, going back into the client's past to better understand what is happening in the present.

The Therapist

Skilled neo-Rogerian therapists cannot be produced through courses in therapeutic technique; they cannot acquire the requisite gifts by reading how-to books on experiential therapy. The foundation must be philosophic and personal rather than technical. Rogers (1951) outlined these qualities of a therapist.

> The primary point of importance here is the attitude held by the counselor toward the worth and the significance of the individual. How do we look upon others? Do we see each person as having worth and dignity in his own right? If we do hold this point of view at the verbal level, to what extent is it operationally evident at the behavioral level? Do we tend to treat individuals as persons of worth, or do we subtly devaluate them by our attitudes and behavior? Is our philosophy one in which respect for the individual is uppermost? Do we respect his capacity and his right to self-direction, or do we basically believe that his life would be best guided by us? To what extent do we have a need and a desire to dominate others? Are we willing for the individual to select and choose his own values, or are our actions guided by the conviction (usually unspoken) that he would be happiest if he permitted us to select for him his values and standards and goals? (p. 20)

The philosophic orientation of the therapist must, then, be compatible with both phenomenology and a belief in the innate capacity of humankind for growth and adaptation. When good skills implement that philosophic stance, the possibility for success is enhanced. By the same token, if therapists have the proper orientation only, their intentions may be good but they may not be sufficiently facilitative once they have acquired the necessary skills. Many people, for instance, are born with artistic ability, but not all of them become artists. Conversely, a person with minimal intrinsic ability can be taught some competence in sketching. When a natural talent is nurtured by training in the discipline to bring about full expression of that talent, then we have an artist. And when a therapist with an instinctive respect for the worth and dignity of each individual acquires the techniques for sophisticated expression of this philosophy, then we have a fully functioning therapist. As Rogers (1951) put it, "the counselor who is effective in client-centered therapy holds a coherent and developing set of attitudes deeply imbedded in his personal organization, a system of attitudes which is implemented by techniques and methods consistent with it" (p. 19).

Who, then, is qualified to provide experiential psychotherapy? Does one need to be a psychoanalyst or to have a doctorate in psychology? Rogers felt not.

> It is *not* stated that special intellectual professional knowledge—psychological, psychiatric, medical, or religious—is required of the therapist. (The conditions) which apply especially to the therapist are qualities of experience, not intellectual information. If they are to be acquired, they must, in my opinion, be acquired through an experiential training—which may be, but usually is not, a part of professional

training. . . . Intellectual training and the acquiring of information has, I believe, many valuable results—but becoming a therapist is not one of those results. (1957, 101)

Many members of the psychotherapeutic community have distorted this belief of Roger's, suggesting that he is giving license to unskilled people to practice therapy. The truth is that experiential therapy requires a high degree of skill, but not necessarily skill acquired in formal education. Some contend that only highly trained analysts should practice uncovering analysis, but that therapists who have not had such intense training, can do supportive/relationship therapy, because even if they do no good, they will do no harm. Unfortunately, the data do not reinforce this. We do have data (Truax and Mitchell 1968) showing that therapists who practice relationship therapy without the presence of the good conditions for a therapeutic relationship do, in fact, cause their clients to get worse. When the good conditions are absent or diminished, the client's condition may well worsen.

The qualities that children like in a therapist may also help us identify the effective child therapist. Bonner and Everett (1982, in press) examined children's attitudes and expectations of psychotherapy. One question they asked of six- to twelve-year-old children was, "What kind of therapist would you like to see?" The children responded with various descriptors of characteristics that are currently thought to be associated with successful treatment. The children frequently mentioned that they would like to see a therapist who was "nice, helpful, friendly, understanding, and good." Other, less frequently used descriptors included "open-minded," "experienced," "warm," "gentle," "strict," "not strict," "patient," "trustworthy," "talkative," "one who doesn't yell," "one who won't laugh at me," "one who doesn't get angry," and "one who will explain things." Many of these descriptors may be subsumed under the framework of warmth, genuineness, and empathy developed by Rogers and his colleagues (Truax and Carkhuff 1967).

Misinterpretations of the Therapist's Role

Rogers and his colleagues noted as early as 1957 that the nondirective, reflecting style of client-centered therapy could easily be misused; they apparently felt that a lack of congruence was the major pitfall. Speaking of client-centered therapy, Rogers described it as being "open to the pitfall of a rather wooden imitation, a sort of formula behind which a frightened or conflicted, or uninvolved, therapist could hide. The reflection formula of 'You feel . . .' might look good on a transcript, but in action it could vary from a deep response to an artificial front."

To avoid this pitfall, and thus to become a more genuine therapist, one must respond to nonverbal cues as much as or more than to verbal ones. And the therapist must respond to affect more than to content. He or she must be willing to take a stand or make a commitment, whereas the stereotypical therapist would depend only on technique, responding to and reflecting only the content of the client's communication:

Mark: I can't go on.
Therapist: You've had it?
Mark: Yes, I just can't do this any longer.
Therapist: You've come to the end of your rope.
Mark: Yes, but what's wrong with the way I say it?

Noncommittal treatment by a therapist who simply repeats content might be equally effective if performed by a parrot who had been taught to say What do *you* think about it? That, of course, is not what any form of supportive therapy is or ever has been. But particularly since the Wisconsin experiments, it is even farther removed from the ideal. With the increased emphasis on congruence, it is now almost impossible to read verbatim accounts of therapy and determine whether the therapist is Rogerian or not, because Rogerian techniques will often resemble those of the transference-conscious or dynamically oriented therapist. Fiedler (1950) has shown that there is a greater difference between a skilled and unskilled therapist of a given orientation than there is between skilled therapists of different orientations. The difference between Rogerian and non-Rogerian therapy is in the orientation, in the motivations that lead to the style, rather than to the content that can be superficially read in a transcript. There are subtle differences in therapy which do not immediately meet the eye but which can be felt by the client at some level. Small, subtle, almost imperceptible expressions, for example, of respect for the self-determination, the locus of responsibility, and the rights of the client may not appear obvious in a verbatim transcript, but they do make a difference.

The wooden, stereotypical, or parrot-like response of an unskilled client-centered therapist may suggest a lack of understanding of this approach. It indicates a bending over backward not to violate the client's right to self-determination when, in fact, nondirective therapy can be extremely directive. When it follows a post-Wisconsin style, it is directive in that the therapist refuses to take over for the client and says so. For example, if a client asks, "Should I run away from home?" the therapist would *not* say, "What do you think about it?" (as some less-directive types might). Rather, the therapist would simply explain directly that he or she could not give an answer because it would require a takeover and would thus violate the principle of locus of responsibility. Thus the therapist is highly direct in the manner in which he or she responds.

Experiential therapy is also directive inasmuch as it insists that the focus of attention be the emotions or current experience of the client rather than the content of the conversation. The skilled therapist is always focusing on affect and, by using that focus, is in a sense insisting that the subject of the therapy hour be the child's feelings. Essentially, the therapist says, You can talk about anything you wish, but I am only going to respond to feelings. This de facto nature of client-centered therapy has been documented by Truax (1966). The directing effect of such styles is clear, and on that level "nondirective" therapy is anything but nondirective.

Nonverbal Communication

Attention to a child's feelings may require that much time be spent in silence. As in Wisconsin, the therapist may find himself or herself expressing personal feelings, since those of the child are not available for attention; this is another opportunity to manifest the therapist's congruent, honest expression of what is going on inside the client, and to model behavior that he or she hopes will be of value to the child.

The experiential therapist will view such silences as opportunities for client and therapist to *feel* together rather than to *think* together and will know how to use these times to nurture intimacy. In instances where a client insists on responding with thoughts rather than with feelings, the therapist may state (congruently) a preference that the two of them *feel* together. In the spirit of the Rogerian tradition, this congruent expression must be offered on a take-it-or-leave-it basis. Such a suggestion may be ignored by the client or pursued, should the client choose to do so. From our experience, such an opportunity will be used by the client for growth; one hopes the client will come to consider the therapy hour as a time for feeling more than talking. The client's manner will become more relaxed when he or she realizes that it is not necessary to "produce" or to "be interesting" for the therapist.

Frustrations of Working with Children

Because of the differences between children and adults as clients, therapy with children will cause frustrations not encountered with adults. Unlike adult patients, who often give effusive praise to therapists who do not warrant it, children are often nonverbal—they seldom express appreciation for their therapists. There will be very few other indications of success to encourage therapists who work with children; at the end of a therapy hour, they may wonder whether the session was worthwhile at all. Therapists who still need verbal reassurances of success will not find them in therapy with children, and if they still need to feel that they are "practicing therapy" in a stereotypic fashion, they will be frustrated in working with children, particularly in experiential therapy. The stereotype of what therapy is and the reality of what actually happens between a skilled therapist and a child are miles apart. The most effective therapist who spends a productive hour with a child may do nothing that conforms to the usual process of adult therapy. Often there is no psychological jargon, no insightful dialogue right out of the textbook. The "Aha, now I understand" moments occur only once in a blue moon in experiential therapy with children, although they may appear five or six times on a single textbook page. There will be long periods of silence and moments of frustration which will make the therapist wonder if anything constructive is happening. But therapy is more than just playing with a child. If it were not, any warm and agile adult could do the job. Wanting to help children is not enough; effective therapy with a child requires a sound attitudinal and philosophic base combined with the highest level of interpersonal skills and discipline, and comes from patience.

Another source of the frustration encountered with children is the lack of feedback or of visible, tangible evidence that change is occurring. Adults tend to tell the therapist when they are getting better, but children are often unaware of their progress, or if they know of it, they seldom feel obliged to share this information. In such a situation, a therapist who lacks a firm internal locus of evaluation might be tempted to distort the therapy by asking for feedback or by probing for some verbal psychological expression on which to base a feeling that improvement is really taking place. An insecure therapist who cannot tolerate periods of silence and minimal responses might be tempted to abandon experiential therapy.

Parents may become a problem for the therapist when the child begins to improve, if the improvement manifests itself in a style that does not appeal to them. A passive, unresponsive child may improve to the point that he or she may tell a sibling to "bug off." From a parent's perspective, this may not be an improvement, even though the skilled therapist recognizes the behavior as a clumsy but necessary step both in the development of a client's ability to recognize and handle inner experience and in the improvement of interpersonal skills.

Because children are reluctant to show change or to verbalize feelings, the impact of therapy is often greater than the therapist realizes. This is frequently revealed by a child's delayed reaction to a statement the therapist may have thought had gone unheeded; weeks, even months later, the child brings it up and comments on it as though it had been made only a few moments before. This suggests that in the intervening time the topic had been on the child's mind, affecting thoughts, and behavior.

The Child

The first step in the process of seeking help for a child is deciding that the child needs special care. Children are typically brought to therapy by their parents, or they are referred for help by teachers, pediatricians, or others who are responsive enough to the child's difficulties to make the difficult decision to seek assistance. Parents and other concerned adult caretakers carry around with them norms for evaluating the appropriateness of a child's behavior. Such norms are not clear and concise, however, and the assessment of normal and abnormal behavior is a complicated and socially relative process. Problems must be assessed multidimensionally within the context of such factors as the child's age, intellectual development, physical development, environment, culture, ethnic group, and the level of the parent's tolerance. Allowances must always be made for individuality. Referral decisions are also complicated by the normal variability of children's behavior. Parents try to decide when a problem is worse than the usual ups and downs of childhood. Others who know the child may be unsure at first about their decision to seek professional assistance.

Assessment and Psychodiagnostic Evaluation of the Child

Professionals use assessments and psychodiagnostic evaluations to identify children who need specialized care or therapy. Formal diagnostic methods or testing may be necessary to determine whether genetic or organic factors are involved; they may also be of some value in pinpointing the nature and severity of psychopathology. This diagnosis is in turn useful in predicting the extent of therapy needed and the chances for its success. Testing is also typically required to determine psychoeducational placement or progress. However, formal testing to provide dynamic insights into the nuances of a client's presumably pathologic behavior is not useful for experiential psychotherapists. Extended relationship therapy provides the best insights. Since the therapist is following a client-determined course in therapeutic interaction and is otherwise adhering to the principle that the locus of responsibility is in the client, he or she does not need test results to produce desirable dynamic insights.

To identify those children in need of special help or therapy, assessments of certain criteria may also be useful (Everett 1983).

1. How are the parents and child feeling? Perhaps there is a perception that the child is not happy, not fitting in, not learning, or not actualizing him or herself. When parents feel that something is wrong, help may be needed. The child's feelings and the child's reality are also most important. Is the child worried, anxious, fearful, or despondent? If the problems matter to the child and the child is suffering, intervention is appropriate.

Feelings and perceptions of self are also good indicators of the child's level of adjustment. The self-actualizing or fully functioning person accepts his or her own nature. Such an individual can accept both strong and weak personality traits and has a positive total view of self. The child who does not like or accept self may benefit from therapy.

2. How severe are the symptoms? The nature, frequency, intensity, and duration of symptoms are relevant to decisions on referral. More severe symptoms, such as excessive physical aggression, obviously require more immediate attention. In general, the more problems the child experiences, the greater the severity of the disturbance, and the greater the need for special care.

Problems must also be assessed in terms of the extent to which they interfere with the child's growth and development. Some difficulties, such as school phobia or poor peer relations, are likely to adversely affect the child's development in many ways. The consequences of these problems are severe, so the problems should receive attention.

3. How persistent have the child's problems been? Transient fluctuations in behavior are common in children. At times it is useful to "wait and see" and to give the child time to find his or her own solution. We would not, for example, become overly concerned with a child who occasionally does not want to go to school or who is briefly despondent. When time has passed, however, and improvements are not noted, additional efforts may be appropriate. When problems persist despite efforts of the child and others to effect change, we become more concerned. In general, the more persistent the child's problems over time, the greater the need for intervention.

4. Is the child's behavior age-appropriate? Behavior varies as a function of age, and many behaviors are normal at one age but not at another. What may be a problem for a 12-year-old may not be a problem for a 2-year-old and vice versa. For example, a temper tantrum or separation anxiety in a 2-year-old will not give rise to serious concern. We would, however, be more concerned about a 12-year-old who exhibits similar behavior. While there are no rigid rules, there are general expectations as to the timing of many aspects of development. A child's problems must be interpreted within a developmental framework. When

behavior is not age-appropriate, and whenever a child's problems interfere with growth and development, there is cause for concern.

5. Does the child have satisfactory social relationships with other children and adults? We live in a social environment in which meaning and satisfaction emanate from interaction with others. The fully functioning or adequate person is comfortable with others and is capable of maintaining healthy and warm personal relationships. Such individuals find it easy to accept and relate to others. Developing and maintaining satisfactory social relationships is, thus, one measure of personal adjustment. The child with unsatisfactory social relationships is missing an important part of childhood. Social restrictions may prevent the child from doing many things that could be enjoyable.

6. How is the child's behavior affecting those around him or her? We live in a complex social network where the behavior of one may affect many. A child's aggressiveness may, for example, directly inflict pain on others. An overly aggressive child needs assistance for the sake of him or herself as well as for the sake of the victim. While problems of acting-out behavior are more likely to be noted, more passive, withdrawn behaviors may also adversely affect others. Concern is warranted whenever a child's behavior adversely affects others.

Answers to the preceding questions may help identify those children who could benefit from therapy. Again, one must remember that the felt reality of the child and the parents is more relevant than what the therapist perceives in these or more formal diagnostic categories.

Children in Treatment

An accurate determination of the incidence of emotional disturbance in children is difficult. Estimates vary with the definition of disturbance, the agencies sampled (schools, child guidance centers, residential hospitals), and the identification methods. We can conclude that large numbers of children experience problems in living that are serious enough to warrant professional attention. A report prepared for the Joint Commission on the Mental Health of Children (Glidewall and Swallow 1968) indicated that 30 percent of elementary school youth showed at least mild adjustment problems and 10 percent needed professional clinical assistance. The common estimate that over the course of one year 10 percent of all children experience disruptive emotional disorders is probably conservative (Rutter 1975; Clarizio and McCoy 1976). Unfortunately, the needs of many of these children are not being adequately met; only a small proportion of disturbed youngsters receives any kind of treatment (President's Commission on Mental Health 1978; Zigler 1974). A "crisis in child mental health care" clearly exists (Joint Commission on Mental Health of Children 1970).

Emotional disturbance is not randomly distributed throughout the childhood population. Descriptions of children in therapy suggest that some children are more likely than others to be at risk. Behavioral and emotional disturbance in childhood is, for instance, largely a male phenomenon; boys outnumber girls for almost every major referral problem. Studies on sex differences indicate that boys are approximately three times more likely than girls to be referred for emotional or behavioral disorders (Clarizio and McCoy 1976; Erickson 1978). While this ratio does change following adolescence, boys are still more likely to be referred for therapy. There are no definitive explanations for such statistics, but it may be that both genetic and environmental factors play a role in the greater vulnerability of boys.

While children's illnesses are individual, unique cases, the most common diagnosis reported has been adjustment reaction or transient situational disorder. Although this suggests that many childhood disturbances are brief and transitory, such an interpretation should be made cautiously. Since difficulties inherent in diagnostic classification are often coupled with reluctance to label children, it is difficult to describe reliably the types of problems that affect children of various ages. Although we may acknowledge a most common diagnosis, children come to therapy with diverse problems.

Descriptions of children in treatment are valuable in defining the average client. Within the clinic, however, we work with individual children with individualized problems, so our approaches in therapy are designed for unique individuals.

The Child as a Client

Experiential therapists are primarily concerned with the experiential condition of the child. Their emphasis is on providing the good conditions of intimacy, congruence, valuing, empathy and responsibility, and on seeing what the children can *become,* without preconceived bias as to what they should be. Familiarization with theories of child development is, however, important if the therapist is to understand the natural progressions of development. Such knowledge can also enable the therapist to relate better to the child client. In view of the developmental differences between children and adults and between children of different ages, age-specific intervention or therapeutic strategies have been created. Child therapies or play therapies, for example, have evolved to meet the unique needs of children.

Children in treatment are highly dependent on their environment and their parents. Since children must have their basic needs met by adults, they are especially vulnerable to environmental stresses; this generalized dependency affects their psychotherapy. Clearly, children rely on parents to initiate the treatment process, to bring them to sessions, and to pay the bills. Moreover, the course of therapy is influenced by the quality of parental attitudes and support. Because of this dependence on parents, therapy with children often includes collaboration with parents or other significant adults.

Also, children in treatment are not usually the applicants, but are made to come to therapy by their parents. These children may be troubling to their parents rather than to themselves. Such clients may have little motivation to begin relating to the therapist, while other children may realize that they feel troubled but may still have little motivation for engaging in the therapeutic process. The awareness of therapeutic possibilities requires more advanced conceptual development. Thus, the child's perception of the problem and its solution is frequently different from the parents' perception.

In therapy, the young child may perceive the therapist as being big and powerful. Indeed, the therapist may be more powerful than parents since they, too, go to the therapist for help; children are brought to therapy only after parents or other adults have admitted that their help is not sufficient. Such decisions are not made lightly and are accompanied by frustration. The child may anticipate that therapy, too, will be frustrating and that the therapist will be fearsome, disapproving, or punitive. For children who have special problems in relating to the therapist, the conditions of intimacy, congruence, valuing, empathy, and responsibility will be especially important.

The child's cognitive and linguistic development also vary as a function of age, so an understanding of age and stage aspects of language and cognition can improve the therapist's ability to communicate with the child. For the child, the preschool years are years of language mastery. The first words begin to appear in infancy, and their emergence introduces a stage of rapid language development. By the time the child enters elementary school, his or her vocabulary has expanded greatly, the informal rules of language have been almost mastered, and articulation is near adult level. Such children, though, still have difficulty putting into words many of the feelings, attitudes, and impulses that are relevant to therapy. Because of their limited language skills, young children frequently find it easier to "play out" rather than "talk out" issues. Communication with young children clearly needs to be geared to their level of language development.

Language development is also a part of children's more general cognitive development. The work of Piaget (1969) suggests that children's cognitive development evolves in qualitatively distinct stages. The young child (ages 0–2 years) is characterized as a sensorimotor processor. The preoperational age child (ages 2–7 years) is mastering language; the concrete operational child (ages 7–11 years) develops and demonstrates more flexible and solid, or logical, thought processes. It is only with adolescence and formal operational thought (ages 11–15 years) that there develops the ability to fully grasp the abstractions, such as feelings and one's role as a social stimulus to others, that are so vital to adult forms of psychotherapy. See Piaget (1983) for a more detailed discussion of Piagetian concepts.

Such cognitive developments have clear implications for the style of communication used in therapy. These norms should not, however, suggest standards for the ways children should act and progress in therapy. Instead, an understanding of the work of age and stage theorists such as Piaget can help therapists to understand how children think and to decide how best to relate to them.

The Nature of the Child

Just as the child-centered therapist approaches each case with a preestablished phenomenologic view of the nature of reality, so does he or she also bring a preformed complementary concept of the nature of the child. Broadly speaking, concepts regarding the innate nature of human beings can be divided into three points of view: people are innately good, people are innately bad, or people are innately neutral (neither good nor bad).

The concept of innate neutrality is rooted in the philosophy of John Locke, specifically in his *Essay concerning Human Understanding,* in which he proposes that all ideas are placed in the mind by experience. A child, then, is born a tabula rasa, a blank tablet to be written upon. Behavior theory can trace its philosophic history to this concept.

The concept of innate badness was eloquently presented by John Calvin, whose religious views were predicated on the idea that people are born in sin. He refers to children's "innate perversity" and indicates that we must "bend their natural inclinations and instill good habits and pious thoughts." In contemporary personality theory, this is expressed in orthodox Freudianism, which suggest that children have innate tendencies toward incest and murder, have a pure id, and eventually experience Oedipal impulses, which are curbed only by the development of the ego and super ego.

Contrasting with these two theories is the philosophy expounded by Jean Jacques Rousseau in *The Social Contract,* in which he argued that in a state of nature, isolated and without language, humanity was instinctively good. It was as they began to live together in society that human beings became evil, developing inclinations toward aggressiveness and selfishness. Rousseau's view that people are innately good agrees with the concept of an innate tendency toward growth and adaptation ("fully functioning" status) promoted by modern "self" theorists such as Rogers. This idea is expanded by some to suggest that the human organism has an inborn capacity to heal itself when injured either physically or psychologically; together these concepts form the basis for experiential psychotherapy with children.

Unlike early Protestant reformers and contemporary Freudians, experiential therapists do not seek to counteract evil. Neither do they assume, as do most behavior therapists, that they are treating only learned aberrations that are influenced neither positively nor negatively by the organism itself.

Considerations of Therapy with Children

The Application of Experiential Psychotherapy with Children

Axline's (1947) work applied psychotherapeutic techniques to work with children; Dorfman's (1951) work adapted the later client-centered developments of the period between 1950 and 1957 to psychotherapy with children. But even after the publication of many books translating those experiences into work with adults, the newer experiential approach has not been adapted to psychotherapy with children. Some might argue that Moustakas's *Existential Child Therapy* (1965) or Axline's later (1968) writings meet this need, but the Wisconsin insights on congruence are not clearly integrated into these works. Also, the many works on client-centered therapy in general which have appeared in the last twenty years have been conspicuous in their lack of applicability to psychotherapy with children.

Changes in supportive/relationship psychotherapy brought about by the work of Rogers and his colleagues in Wisconsin clearly have many important implications for therapy with children. Psychotic adults tend to be passive, nonverbal, and seemingly unmotivated in therapy, but they are tuned in to phoniness and can sense when a therapist is saying one thing but feeling another. Since children also can sense insincerity, the changes brought on by the Wisconsin experience appear to have a unique applicability for work with children.

Conditions for Constructive Personality Change in Children

Axline (1947) outlined basic principles that are appropriate for anyone working with children.

> 1. The therapist must develop a warm, friendly relationship with the child, in which good rapport is established as soon as possible.

2. The therapist accepts the child exactly as he or she is.
3. The therapist establishes a feeling of permissiveness in the relationship so that the child feels free to express his or her feelings completely.
4. The therapist is alert to recognize the *feelings* the child is expressing and reflects those feelings back in such a manner that he or she gains insight into behavior.
5. The therapist maintains a deep respect for the child's ability to solve problems if given an opportunity to do so. The responsibility to make choices and to institute change is the child's.
6. The therapist does not attempt to direct the child's actions or conversation in any manner. The child leads the way; the therapist follows.
7. The therapist does not attempt to hurry the therapy along. It is a gradual process and is recognized as such by the therapist.
8. The therapist establishes only those limitations that are necessary to anchor the therapy to the world of reality and to make the child aware of his or her own responsibility in the relationship. (p. 75–76)

In 1957, Rogers set down six conditions he believed to be both necessary and sufficient for therapy with adults to be effective.

For constructive personality change to occur, it is necessary that these conditions exist and continue over a period of time:
1. Two persons are in psychological contact.
2. The first, whom we shall term the client, is in a conspicuous state of incongruence, being vulnerable or anxious.
3. The second person, whom we shall term the therapist, is congruent or integrated in the relationship.
4. The therapist experiences unconditional positive regard for the client.
5. The therapist experiences an empathic understanding of the client's frame of reference and endeavors to communicate this experience to the client.
6. The communication to the client of the therapist's empathic understanding and unconditional positive regard is to a minimal degree achieved.
No other conditions are necessary. If these six conditions exist, and continue over a period of time, this is sufficient. The process of constructive personality change will follow. (p. 96)

We believe that the conditions necessary for constructive personality change within a *child* differ in emphasis from Roger's original conditions. For instance, the child need not be "in a conspicuous state of incongruence, being vulnerable or anxious." Most children, because they are in early stages of cognitive or intellectual development, are not aware of their inner feelings; children brought to therapy often do not feel they are acting maladaptively. Their parents or teachers may believe it, but not necessarily the children themselves. While anxiety, incongruence, or vulnerability may sometimes speed the changes, they are not felt to be prerequisites for change.

The concept that the locus of responsibility resides within each person is not stated separately by Rogers as a necessary condition to change, but it is implied in the other conditions. Rogers's terms *unconditional positive regard, locus of evaluation,* and *nonpossessive warmth* all imply that the client will be responsible for self and that the therapist will respect that responsibility. The goal of communicating this idea to the child is often accomplished by what the therapist does *not* do more than by what he or she does do. This concept seems important enough in child therapy to warrant its emphasis as a separate condition.

Rogers's necessary and sufficient conditions, translated for the purposes of this text, can now be enumerated as follows:

1. The child and the helper are in intimate psychological contact.
2. The helper is congruent in the relationship.
3. The helper experiences and communicates unconditional positive regard for the child.
4. The helper experiences the child's internal frame of reference empathically and communicates that empathy to the child.
5. The helper requires that the locus of responsibility for the child's behavior be vested in the child.

The Goal of Therapy

For the experiential therapist, the goal of psychotherapy is to remove barriers to the natural unfolding of the self-actualizing capability within each child. Any specific goals for therapeutic gain, such as increased task effectiveness, more appropriate interpersonal functioning as defined by parent or teacher, less affective discomfort, or freedom from symptoms, are avoided. The therapist hopes, of course, that the child's effect on others will change, that behavior will become more adaptive as judged by the therapist and other observers, that the child will profess to be happier, and that there will be other objective evidence of more integrated functioning (e.g., better grades in school). But the therapist has no way of knowing if any of these changes will occur, or what specific events may trigger them. Specific goals, then, are viewed as possible sources of limitation to the unique potentialities of each child and thus are undesirable. The therapist must be concerned with removing the barriers to that child's growth and letting the child's own capacity for growth, the forward thrust, the healing potential, indicate the direction that is right for that child.

The experiential psychotherapist usually harbors the bias that affect precedes cognition, that is, that changes in feelings produce changes in thinking, rather than vice versa. Like Hobbs (1962), he or she feels that insight is a consequence rather than an antecedent of therapeutic change. The therapist's goal, then, is to provide a climate that alters the child's affect, which in turn will change the child's thinking. The goal is to proceed without employing logic or interpretation, in the hope of influencing the child's thinking in a manner that may eventually allow the child to feel better.

The Stages of Therapy

In the evolution of psychotherapy with children, three stages are repeatedly observed. The first is the establishment of intimacy, which is accomplished for the most part by the therapist's being empathic, genuine, nonpossessive, and warm. This is the foundation for any change, and little can be expected to occur in the therapeutic relationship without it. The second stage is reached when the child begins symbolically expressing feelings that were previously stifled (e.g., aggression, dependency, lack of self-esteem, or insufficient feelings of self-acceptance). At the third stage, the child becomes more congruent within his or her own level of growth (see Congruence, in Chapter 3). At this stage, even a child who is not ready or emotionally mature enough to advance to any appreciable level of either self-awareness or self-disclosure will, to the extent that he or she is capable, become more genuine, expressing feelings with words rather than with symbols or actions.

This progression is most difficult to chart in very young children. How can we tell when a child of four has reached the third stage? As an illustration, let us presume that in the early stages of therapy, the 4-year-old's behavior would be viewed by many as an attempt to get attention by being silly and showing off. The child may be substituting such activity for more appropriate expressions of affect and may actually be discharging feelings of anxiety via these techniques. Greater calmness, casualness, spontaneity, and more direct or genuine expressions of affect would indicate that the child has progressed toward the third level. With an older child, recognizing this third stage of therapy is simpler. An older child may be mature enough actually to express feelings verbally by saying such things as (to quote one client), "I don't want to be dependent on my parents any longer. That lets them get their hooks into me, you know, tell me what to do all the time. I'm ready to be my own person."

Similarities and Differences between the Child and the Severely Disturbed Adult

Psychotherapists who work with children should be exceptionally secure individuals who have confidence in their skills; particularly, they should possess an internal locus of evaluation. Such qualities are required because of the similarities between young clients and psychotic clients such as those treated by Rogers and his co-workers in Wisconsin.

The Wisconsin group observed that, regardless of the degree of understanding, acceptance, and genuineness offered by therapists, schizophrenic patients tended to perceive a relatively low level of these conditions existing in a relationship; only slowly over the course of therapy did they perceive more of these attitudes from their therapists. With these severely disturbed adults, then, therapists could be empathic, warm, and genuine but might not be given credit for such by the client. This same frustration appears in therapy with children. Rogers et al. (1967) noted four characteristics of severely disturbed adults which are often found in children: silence; the absence of an exploration process; the absence of a self-propelled process; and rejection of the therapist.

Children, like severely disturbed adults, are less comfortable focusing on self-exploration than are mildly disturbed adults. Rogers et al. (1967) said that "our schizophrenic patients exhibited in general a very low level of involvement in the process of change, and were decidedly remote from their own experience. They also showed a very limited degree of movement on the instruments we devised for measuring stages of therapeutic process" (p. 79). Most clinicians who are experienced with both adults and children would say that a similar tendency exists in children. One of the factors that drives many therapists away from psychotherapy with children is the frustration of being unable to use verbal-intellectual techniques and therefore having to rely solely on relationship variables, which are vague and imprecise.

Children are, of course, quite different from schizophrenic adults. The evidence shows that there is more hope for response and growth from children than from schizophrenics. The cognitive and affective styles of individuals who have yet to mature are obviously different from those of adults who matured but then regressed. Disturbed adults tend to live in an inner world, shutting out external stimulation and responding primarily to internal stimulation. Children, unless they are severely disturbed, tend to be more involved with the external world, although normal development of children does include considerable response to their inner world and fantasy. Early in their ontogenic development, children also tend, but to a lesser degree than do psychotics, to maintain an egocentric view of the world. Children's lack of contact with reality may stem from their being in an early stage of conceptual development, whereas with disturbed adults, the perceptions are distorted and lead to delusional concepts. The plasticity of children is, it is hoped, another important difference. Because the clients are being reached early, there is a greater likelihood that these positive experiences will bring them significant and lasting improvement.

3

Interpersonal Conditions for Therapeutic Gain

Intimacy

> Gradually I have come to the conclusion that one
> learning which applies to all of these experiences is
> that it is the quality of personal relationship which
> matters most. With some of these individuals I
> am in touch only briefly, with others I have the
> opportunity of knowing them intimately, but in
> either case the quality of the personal encounter is
> probably, in the long run, the element which
> determines the extent to which this is an experi-
> ence which releases or promotes development and
> growth.
>
> —Rogers, Some Learnings from a Study of
> Psychotherapy with Schizophrenics

The initial focus of the therapist must be directed toward establishing an intimate relationship with the child, since intimacy is the medium in which therapeutic growth occurs. This atmosphere can best be characterized as a feeling of
safety; it has been described as a state in which one person knows and cares
about another, but by virtue of what he or she is, demands that the other be true
to self. In the relationship between therapist and child, the child feels safe
enough to disclose self, revealing strengths and weaknesses. Rogers (1957) de-
scribes intimacy as *relationship:* the client and therapist are *in relationship.* When

this condition exists, more spontaneous behavior replaces calculated, deliberate acts, and the child no longer feels the need to weigh words for fear of rejection or misunderstanding. The child understands that here he or she is deeply accepted and understood.

Every experiential therapist understands that in the early stages of therapy he or she and the client will begin to develop a special feeling for one another as well as a special feeling about their time together. This relationship involves trust, understanding, warmth, and closeness; the child feels and behaves differently in this more nurturing environment. For instance, after intimacy has been achieved, a therapist can say things to a child that would have been inappropriate before. He or she can express negative emotions and can even be demanding without making the child feel rejected. This could never have been risked in earlier stages of therapy, but once a high level of relationship has been established, such manifestations of intimacy can be ventured.

The Importance of Intimacy

To understand the importance of such intimacy for the child, one must remember those few special relationships that profoundly changed one's own life. In these relationships, whether they were called a special friendship or love, a person related differently, felt profoundly, and disclosed self on a deep level. The highly significant other person may have been a parent or a peer, but if one has had such a relationship, one always remembers the feeling of safety and the nourishment found in that trusting association. Most likely, the relationship paralleled a period of personal reorganization much like the one desired for the client. Such an atmosphere is one of the good conditions the therapist must strive to create. In this atmosphere of trust the child will be free to grow and heal.

When there is no intimacy, people tend to rigidify and become defensive, resorting to sameness rather than risking a new way of being. Only when children are freed from defending self can they become flexible enough to permit change, to consciously think previously unacknowledged thoughts, and to speak of previously taboo subjects. There are clusters of personal topics which will only be discussed by children in an atmosphere of safety, particularly topics relating to sex, negative emotions, self-doubt, and even positive feelings about self.

The ability of children to tolerate, experience, and promote intimacy will have extensive influence on all their future relationships—sexual, marital, and filial—and will affect their life's work and future parenting. Parents incapable of intimacy may inadvertently influence their children's future interpersonal style by their model, creating similar styles in their offspring.

One consequence of a lack of intimacy during early development is increased vulnerability to what has been termed existential neurosis. This increasingly encountered form of psychopathology is characterized by lack of meaning and purpose in life, lack of identity, lack of direction, a feeling of estrangement from other people and from the world in general, and, usually, depression of varying intensity. This cluster of traits seems closely tied to the presence or absence of intimacy; thus, children who have not experienced intimacy or who cannot tolerate it are more susceptible in later years to existential conflicts.

Indications of Intimacy

One obvious indication of intimacy is the content of the therapy hour. If a bond has been established, the child's responses will be less superficial; genuineness may take the form of greater self-disclosure, or it may simply result in the child's feeling comfortable with silence for the first time. A verbal child will discuss topics that are not discussed between mere acquaintances, but only with intimates. This trust may express itself physically as well; the child may become more comfortable making physical contact with the therapist. He or she may look at the therapist directly rather than avoid eye contact, and may even change his or her tone of voice, reflecting a more relaxed, personal, genuine attitude. Body positions, dress, even speaking style, will reflect the degree of comfort and trust. Indications of change may be subtle with less verbal children, manifesting themselves not through verbalized insights but rather through what Rogers (1951) characterized as "a fresh and vital experiencing of self" (p. 158).

Fostering Intimacy

Touching can be an excellent means of fostering intimacy, especially with children who are reluctant to talk—an arm around the shoulder can communicate that they are valued and that they are in a safe place. Touching adult patients, especially those of the opposite sex, is seldom advisable, but with children this is less often a problem. It is usually acceptable to touch the child, and to let the child touch you, within obvious bounds of propriety. The touching must feel natural and comfortable to the therapist, of course, reflecting ease with the contact and liking of the child.

As an example, a graduate student who was seeing an early adolescent boy felt that the therapy was deficient at the point of relationship, that there was no real intimacy; the two of them, he felt, needed to become closer before therapy could progress. When the student reported that he and the child had never touched, his supervisor suggested that he try physical contact as a means of fostering the intimacy he desired. The student agreed that contact would feel comfortable and natural and so decided to try it.

The child and the student therapist always met in a waiting room and walked a hundred feet down a narrow hallway to the therapy room, so the trainee decided that the next time they met, if it felt right, he would put his hand on the boy's shoulder as they walked down the hallway to begin the therapy hour. Afterward, the trainee reported that this simple gesture seemed to make a major difference in the boy's responsiveness and consequently in the therapy session. This, in fact, proved to be a turning point, after which the relationship became more intimate and the *therapy more productive*.

Some very young children can pose a special challenge to one's skills in facilitating intimacy. With young clients, verbal content becomes less meaningful, and what they see or feel is of greater significance.

Christine was a 4-year-old victim of child abuse who had been taken from her natural mother. Her foster parents were given regular coaching sessions on providing good conditions in the home. To supplement this, individual therapy sessions were begun with Christine in order to provide her with experiences akin to warm, effective "mothering." Because she could tolerate very little closeness, her therapist elected to avoid directly intimate talk. He spoke in a soft warm voice and was gentle and complimentary, but at the same time was careful not to force himself upon her. He focused his efforts on what Christine *saw* in him (e.g., a frequent smile, love expressed toward a doll). The therapist began a systematic attempt to desensitize Christine to being touched. The first step was for therapist and client to compare hand sizes, allowing for a brief touch. Hand-touching experiences began with two seconds of touching and doubled in length with each session, up to thirty-two seconds in five sessions. Next the therapist began a "guess your weight" experience in which Christine had to be lifted. The lifting began with a four-second lift and doubled in length each session, up to thirty-two seconds in four sessions.

Finally, Christine having been somewhat desensitized, the therapist began a "test his own strength" program to see how long he could hold the client. This required some special effort in order to be congruent and not phoney. The therapist did not try to act as though he could barely lift the client. Lifting and holding began with ten-second intervals and doubled each session to one minute and twenty seconds in four sessions. After the above experiences were completed, holding and touching became more spontaneous and increased in frequency and duration throughout subsequent sessions. Such experiences seemed to help Christine relate in a warmer, more intimate manner.

On another occasion a child came to therapy with wet pants. Because of the minimal degree to which relationship had been established, she was not willing to discuss her problem. The therapist, however, used the event to indicate his relaxed attitude toward this sensitive issue while at the same time respecting the child's right not to discuss it.

> *Therapist:* I see your pants are wet; that must be uncomfortable. Would you
>   like to go to the bathroom?
> *Mary:* [*No response*]
> *Therapist:* You seem like you don't want to talk about it, and that's okay.

The delicate balance involves indicating the therapist's true comfort with the topic without insisting that the child feel equally comfortable. Discussions of feelings relating to wet pants, sex, fears, anger, abandonment, or even pimples, are not what produce intimacy, but are rather the fruits of it, once it has been established.

Another way to model the trust and safety in a relationship is to avoid euphemisms. Direct talk can foster not only intimacy, but acceptance and congruence as well:

> *Sara:* I had a date last night. We went to a movie and then for a drive. Al
>   stopped the car on this country road and we sat there and made out for
>   awhile. Then it happened. I didn't think it would happen, but sometimes
>   before you know it, it happens. I don't want it to happen, but it does.
> *Therapist:* What you're telling me is, you had intercourse last night.
> *Sara:* Yeah.
> *Therapist:* And having intercourse as often as you do, and when you don't
>   really plan to, frightens you.
> *Sara:* Yeah.
> *Therapist:* There's something about not being in control of your sexual
>   behavior that's scary.

In this instance the therapist's use of the word *intercourse* for *it* suggested that the client's sexual behavior could be discussed in a relaxed rather than frightening atmosphere. Sara had apparently presumed the opposite, because she used a euphemism. Greater client comfort with the topic of sexual behavior would indicate an increasing sense of intimacy.

Disclosures by the therapist of his or her own deep feelings can be another way of fostering intimacy, but these must be made sparingly and with great skill. They should not distract the therapist from concentrating on the child's needs, which must always be the focus of therapy. The therapy is for the child, not for the therapist. It would likely be inappropriate for the therapist to say, "I have phobias, too; I won't fly in an airplane," or, "Don't worry about being afraid of the dark; when I was your age I was afraid of it, too," and then to divert the focus of the hour to a discussion of those fears. It may not be inappropriate, however, for the therapist to say something like: "I understand your fear; I may not have the same fears you have, but there are things I'm afraid of." The test is always whether or not the disclosure is in the service of the child.

Claire was a 13-year-old girl with problems of impulse control. In the past she had performed sadistic acts on animals and other children.

> *Claire:* Last night I babysat. The baby cried a lot and I didn't know what to do. I couldn't get her to stop. Then I saw something at the window. I was afraid someone was gonna come in and hurt the baby.
>
> *Therapist:* Sounds like you had some pretty scary feelings.
>
> *Claire:* Yeah, really scary.
>
> *Therapist:* You were afraid something might happen to the baby.
>
> *Claire:* Well, sorta. I don't know why, but at that moment I felt like I wanted to hurt the baby myself.
>
> *Therapist:* And those feelings of anger and wanting to hurt really amazed you, didn't they?
>
> *Claire:* Yeah.
>
> *Therapist:* Somehow, I'm not surprised by them.
>
> *Claire:* How do you mean?
>
> *Therapist:* Well, for one thing, everyone seems to have them.
>
> *Claire:* [*Disbelievingly*] Really?
>
> *Therapist:* Sounds like you thought you might be the only person who felt that way and that meant there was something wrong with you.
>
> *Claire:* It's just hard to believe.
>
> *Therapist:* That all the other nice people you know have bad thoughts just like you do?
>
> *Claire:* Yeah, what do *you* do?
>
> *Therapist:* I accept them and assume they're normal and try to make sure my behavior's right when I feel like doing things I shouldn't. But I'm not afraid to think or feel bad things.
>
> *Claire:* You sometimes feel like . . . [*pause*].
>
> *Therapist:* Yeah, I sometimes feel like doing terrible things to someone else.
>
> *Claire:* Do other people know that about you?
>
> *Therapist:* Some people do, but I only talk about it to people I'm close to.

Forcing Intimacy

Intimacy cannot be forced. Often, the need of therapists to produce tangible results may dominate and they may push too hard or too soon for disclosures. But relationship cannot be hurried, and if therapists try to force intimacy, they only serve to retard or destroy it. They must always model (exemplify) it, never abandoning depth to superficiality. This requires subtlety and skill; on the one hand, they cannot assume responsibility for their clients' behavior and try to force them to act intimately. On the other hand, therapists must reserve the right to act intimately whether or not their clients choose to respond in kind. Thus, therapists model intimacy and show by trust and transparency that they value and feel safe with the clients.

Chris's mother had put her in an orphanage because a new husband did not want the child. In therapy the child had never said an angry word about her mother or expressed any resentment about having been sent away.

> *Chris:* Mom brought me another Nancy Drew book, but it was one I already had.
> *Therapist:* You seem glad and disappointed at the same time.
> *Chris:* [*Smiling*] I know what you want me to say, but I'm not going to.
> *Therapist:* You've said that a few times today. I feel frustrated and confused when you do, because I don't think I'm expecting you to say anything in particular.

Chris's lack of trust may be the result of a number of factors. She may have brought it with her from a long history of dealing with unreliable or otherwise unsupportive adults, or the therapist may have inadvertently pushed her for disclosure prematurely and put Chris on guard. For whatever reason, the child was not relating intimately, and her smile indicated that she wanted to draw the therapist into an interpersonal "game," which, of course, is incompatible with intimacy. By responding transparently and focusing on what was happening between them, the therapist continued to model intimate behavior while respecting the girl's right to relate as she pleased. The personal disclosure of feelings had no strings attached, so the feelings between them at that moment were not tarnished.

A therapist may often work with children who cannot seem to tolerate intimacy. This is to be expected, since very often children come to therapy in the first place because they have trouble relating intimately with adults. In such instances, the therapist must continue to behave intimately, using whatever behavior he or she believes to be most therapeutic, while at the same time respecting the child's right not to be intimate in return. The therapist must, in effect, say: "It's all right that you aren't comfortable with intimacy right now, but I am still going to be intimate with you and at the same time respect your right not to be intimate with me." This message is never verbalized, but is demonstrated instead. The option of intimacy is always there.

With emotionally impaired children, the therapist may have to be creative and resourceful in finding ways to establish intimacy. Perhaps the strongest, closest, or most intense form of interaction a frightened child can tolerate is simply throwing a ball back and forth, or enjoying a picture book with the therapist, or sharing a soft drink, or watching a squirrel.

When Sam came for therapy, he was seven years old and somewhat autistic in his response to others, and his therapist found it very difficult to reach him. After considerable searching, the therapist determined that the two activities Sam would cooperate in were buying things to eat and watching old buildings being torn down at the medical center where they met. The therapist began to conceptualize the buying of snacks as nurturing and tried as much as possible to make the experience one in which she would "succor" him. She and the client agreed that watching the buildings being destroyed was a secret activity that they would not tell anyone else about. This sharing of a secret seemed to add an element of intimacy to their contact, and it facilitated relating.

Intimacy will come from the therapist's being available and being there in the right way. In effect, the way to foster intimacy or to establish relationship is to skillfully provide the other good conditions necessary for personality reorganization—congruence, valuing, empathy, and client responsibility. Through words, eye contact, tone of voice, and the atmosphere of the therapy hour, the therapist must be empathic and must demonstrate unconditional valuing of the client and respect for the client's right and responsibility of self-determination. Most importantly, the therapist must be genuine, or congruent.

Congruence

> The third condition is that the therapist should be, within the confines of this relationship, a congruent, genuine, integrated person. It means that within the relationship he is freely and deeply himself, with his actual experience accurately represented by his awareness of himself. It is the opposite of presenting a facade, either knowingly or unknowingly.
>
> —Rogers, The Necessary and Sufficient Conditions of Therapeutic Personality Change

The concept of congruence can be understood as a three-level construct. At the first level is simple honesty or genuineness: the therapist is straightforward, not phony. The second stage of congruence involves the therapist's self-awareness. The therapist operating at the first level may be motivated by thoughts and feelings of which he or she is unaware, but at the second stage, such awareness is present. At the third and highest level, the therapist not only understands self, but is willing to be transparent and self-disclosing. This can be invaluable to a child. By disclosing his or her own feelings, the therapist tells the child that he or she is someone who can be trusted with the therapist's feelings; shows how the child's behavior affects other people, and shows that the sessions are a safe place for such disclosure. The therapist models behavior he or she wants the child to imitate.

Therapist: You seem not to want to talk today, and that's okay.
Ruth: [*Age 14, sits in chair ignoring therapist, concentrating on her manicure*]
Therapist: [*After 5 minutes*] I feel a sense of sadness when I'm with you today. I think it's because I sense that you're dissatisfied.
Ruth: I make you sad?
Therapist: Yes.
Ruth: I didn't know I made you feel that way. I wasn't trying to make you sad—well, maybe a little. I wanted to go to a basketball game today, but I had to come here instead.
Therapist: Oh, so you're aggravated at having to come?
Ruth: Yes, it makes me damn mad, as a matter of fact.

In the above example the therapist's self-awareness (level two) and self-disclosure (level three) of the feeling of sadness provided Ruth with valuable data about how she affects others. This implied no rejection, and it served as a model that Ruth seemed to follow in her last comment.

Avoiding Misconceptions

Rogers (1975) realized that the concept of congruence could be misunderstood, and he took pains to explain what it does *not* mean:

> It certainly does not mean that the therapist burdens his client with all of his problems or feelings. It does not mean that he blurts out impulsively any attitude that comes to mind. It does mean, however, that he does not deny to himself the feelings that he is experiencing, and that he is willing to express any persistent feelings that exist in the relationship. It means avoiding the temptation to hide behind a mask of professionalism. (p. 1835)

The criterion for determining when to use congruence is the degree of helpfulness to the child. It is inappropriate for the therapist to express feelings merely for his or her own relief or simply because the feelings exist. The degree of intimacy achieved will largely determine what the therapist should and should not do as regards congruent expressions of personal thoughts and feelings.

Children sense phoniness and will respond in kind. But, the temptation to "make friends" superficially and not get down to business is a common pitfall to genuineness on the therapist's part. In the following example a therapist is having his first meeting with Mary Anne, a 15-year-old girl referred because she had a discipline problem at school. He knows that she is interested in horses.

Therapist: Hello, Mary Anne. I'm Dr. Smith.
Mary Anne: Hi.
Therapist: Would you like to sit down?
Mary Anne: Okay. [*Pause 60–90 seconds*]
Therapist: I understand you're interested in horses.

Both the client and therapist knew they were not there to discuss horses; that Mary Anne's discipline problems were the occasion for the meeting was obvious to both. Thus, a discussion of horses would only lead to an atmosphere of phoniness, lowering the therapist's congruence and credibility from the outset. A better approach might go as follows:

Therapist: Hello, Mary Anne. I'm Dr. Smith.
Mary Anne: Hi.
Therapist: Would you like to sit down?
Mary Anne: Okay. [*Pause*]
Therapist: We both seem to be waiting for the other one to begin.
Mary Anne: I don't have anything to say. You can talk about whatever you like.
Therapist: Well, we've both been asked to this conference by your principal. He's told me you're having some problems with your teachers, and I'd like to get that out in the open.

The preceeding is an example of issues at stake at the first level of congruence—simple genuineness versus phoniness.

Another issue that bears upon the first level of congruence (genuineness) is cheating. It can also touch on the second (self-awareness) and third (self-disclosure) levels as well.

Some children cheat in the course of games used in play therapy. Ignoring obvious cheating distracts from the therapist's genuineness. A therapist ignoring his or her feelings about the cheating is deficient in self-awareness, and a lack of self-disclosure of these feelings may deny the child important data as well as an important model.

Cheating should not be prohibited, but neither should it be ignored. The cheating can be pointed out without accusation or condemnation: "I see that you want to depart from the rules," or "Winning this game must be very important to you." The therapist must be careful not to burden the child with condemnation or value judgments. The word *cheating* is value-laiden and is better left unused for fear of communicating rejection or condemnation.

> *Therapist:* That street is one-way, the opposite way from the direction you're moving.
> *Freddie:* [*Age 9*] It is?
> *Therapist:* Uh huh.
> *Freddie:* You can go any way.
> *Therapist:* Not and stay within the rules.
> *Freddie:* You can too go this way!
> *Therapist:* You *can*, of course, if you wish to change or violate the rules.
> *Freddie:* Can I go this way?
> *Therapist:* Not without changing or violating the rules.
> *Freddie:* That way?
> *Therapist:* Not without changing or violating the rules.
> [*Both patient and therapist then laugh as game proceeds according to the rules*]

The therapist may reach a point where cheating angers him or her because of its constant repetition. If an intimate relationship has been established, he or she might say: "When we set up the rules and agree on them and then you change them, that makes me angry (or it confuses me). Then I don't know where I stand with you." This must be said without rejection. Such information is important feedback to the child about how his or her behavior affects other people, especially those who care about him. The child also learns that someone can be angry and still care.

Effects of the Wisconsin Experience

After the experiences in Wisconsin of Rogers and his associates, congruence emerged as the key therapeutic variable. Prior to these experiences with severely disturbed clients, therapists gave congruence relatively little space in the client-centered literature; in fact, neither congruence nor therapist congruence are even indexed in *Client-centered Therapy* (Rogers 1951). With the publication of *The Therapeutic Relationship and Its Impact* (Rogers et al.) in 1967, congruence acquired new importance and changed the emphasis of therapy in significant ways that can affect work with children.

What happened in Wisconsin? Rogers was there to test his theories on severely disturbed clients, and the initial results were frustrating. Typical of the frustrations was the experience of one therapist seeing a man so disturbed that he was carried into therapy by an attendant, remained in a catatonic stupor throughout the 50-minute session, only to be carried out at the end of the hour. Obviously, there were no feelings to reflect and there was little with which to empathize. The therapists were confounded by experiences such as these, having been accustomed to the bright, verbal, highly motivated clients at the University of Chicago Counseling Center. After sitting through many such frustrating sessions, the therapists came to realize their own incongruity. Although their outward behavior remained calm and accepting, inwardly they were feeling frustrated and sometimes angry, and they were overwhelmed with discouragement and the feeling of exclusion. Finally, in their bafflement, they began to say to their clients such things as: "I want to help, but I really don't feel like I'm of use to you," or "I'm supposed to understand, but I don't feel as if I'm understanding." In revealing themselves, they began providing a model of congruence for schizophrenic clients. By trusting to the point of transparency, they showed the client how to be trusting as well. The therapist's self-disclosure gradually broke through and gave the other a bit of courage to do the same thing.

> *Therapist:* I guess your silence is saying to me that either you don't wish to or can't come out right now, and that's okay, so I won't pester you, but I just want you to know I'm here.
> [*A silence of 17 minutes and 41 seconds follows*]
> *Therapist:* I see I'm going to have to stop in a few minutes.
> [*A silence of 20 seconds*]
> *Therapist:* It's hard for me to know how you've been feeling, but it looks as though part of the time maybe you'd rather I didn't know how you are feeling. Anyway, it looks as though part of the time it just feels very good to let down and relax the tension, but as I say, I really don't know how you feel, it's just the way it looks to me. Have things been pretty bad lately?
> [*A silence of 45 seconds*]
> *Therapist:* Maybe this morning you just wish I'd shut up, and maybe I should, but I just keep feeling, I'd like to, I don't know, be in touch with you in some way.
> [*A silence of 2 minutes and 21 seconds at which point the client yawns*]
> *Therapist:* Sounds discouraged or tired.

Client: No, just lousy.

Therapist: Everything's lousy; now you feel lousy.

[*Then a 39-second silence*]

Therapist: Do you want to come Friday at the usual time?

[*The client yawns and mutters something unintelligible. A 48-second silence*]

Therapist: Just kind of feel sunk way down deep in these lousy feelings, is that something like it?

Client: No.

Therapist: No?

[*Silence of 20 seconds*]

Client: No, I just ain't no good to nobody, never was and never will be.

Therapist: Feeling that, uh, that you're no good to yourself, no good to anybody, never will be any good to anybody. Just that you're completely worthless, uh, those are really lousy feelings, just feel that you're no good at all.

Client: Yeah, that's what this guy I went to town with just the other day told me.

Therapist: This guy that you went to town with really told you that you were no good, is that what you're saying, did I get it right?

Client: Uh, huh.

Therapist: I guess the meaning of that, if I get it right, is that here's somebody that meant something to you, and what does he think of you? Why, he's told you that he thinks you're no good at all, and that just really knocks the props out from under you.

[*Client begins to weep quietly*]

Therapist: And it brings the tears.

[*20 seconds of silence*]

Client: I don't care though.

Therapist: You tell yourself you don't care at all, but somehow I guess part of you cares because some part of you weeps over it.

A Bridge to Other Therapeutic Modes

Congruence is the vehicle through which neo-Rogerian forms of psychotherapy are brought more into harmony with useful methods from other schools of psychotherapeutic thought. We know about the importance of modeling, for instance, from the work of Bandura (1969). Harry Stack Sullivan (1953) and others have shown the value of pointing out examples of transference behavior to the client. Congruence is a device through which the therapist can provide important data for the child concerning his or her impact on others, as has been found beneficial in direct or didactic forms of therapy. Conditioning and behavior-oriented therapists believe that limit-setting has value as a therapeutic tool; acting congruently, the neo-Rogerian therapist can set limits as a way of modeling responsibility. Thus, through congruence, the good tools used in other therapeutic styles can become a part of the good conditions of experiential therapy. All may be used in the service of the child without the therapist's directing the course of therapy or otherwise taking over; rather, they are tools the congruent experiential therapist can use to enhance his or her capacity to create the good conditions in which the child can grow.

Providing Data

In addition to providing a good model, the transparency of the therapist gives the child data that would otherwise be unavailable. By disclosing feelings, the therapist gives feedback as to how the child's actions affect others. This may be new information, and feedback will often be positive and can enhance the child's self-image. Children whose behavior is inappropriate may lack information about how their activities are perceived, and they may over- or underestimate their impact. Whenever a child arouses strong feelings in the therapist, there is a possibility that the child should know how he or she is affecting others.

Todd is a 5-year-old with very little self-control and strong aggressive impulses. In the early therapy sessions, his behavior was overly nice, and he appeared somewhat afraid of the therapist. By the beginning of the second month of treatment, however, Todd is beginning to act out. The therapist congruently sets what she feels are appropriate limits and also congruently discloses her feelings about the child's conduct and its consequences.

> *Todd:* I want to go.
> *Therapist:* [*Empathically at first*] You'd like a change, huh? You seem bored today.
> *Todd:* [*Heading for the door*] No, I just don't like you anymore.
> *Therapist:* It's okay to not like someone or to just be angry. But I can't let you leave. I wouldn't be doing my best if I let you break the rule that we stay together for one hour.
> *Todd:* We aren't together when I go to the bathroom.
> *Therapist:* I feel that's different.
> *Todd:* Well, I need to go to the bathroom.
> *Therapist:* To be honest, I believe you can wait. So, I can't let you go.
> *Todd:* I'll go in my pants.

Therapist: You're wondering if that will make me give in on the rule.

Todd: [*No response*]

Therapist: Well, it won't.

Todd: [*Proceeds to wet his pants a little, possibly because he has a minimally full bladder*]

Therapist: [*No response*]

Todd: You're a bad person and I'm going.

Therapist: [*Places herself in front of the door so as to prevent exit, but does not speak*]

Todd: [*Draws back leg so as to kick the therapist, but hesitates*]

Therapist: In case you're wondering, I won't let you kick me. Not hurting yourself or me while we are together is another rule.

Todd: [*Retreats across the room, then charges and attempts to kick the therapist*]

Therapist: [*Grabs Todd carefully by upper arm so as to stop him, and holds him out at arm's length to prevent the attempted kicks from landing*] I feel it's important for you to know that I won't let you hurt me. In fact, I care about you, so I hope you learn that some other people will try to hurt you if you try to hurt them.

A 15-year-old girl who lives in a children's home is passive and quiet. In therapy, she carelessly handles a delicate plant in the therapist's office, annoying the therapist.

Therapist: It concerns me when you handle the plant. It's not mine and I'm afraid you'll damage it and upset the secretary who takes care of it.

Jan: [*Doesn't say anything but continues to pick at the plant*]

Therapist: You act like you don't have anything you really want to talk about today.

Jan: [*Says nothing, but looks at her watch*]

Therapist: I'm beginning to feel as though you're using the plant to tell me something—something negative that you can't just come right out and say.

Jan: [*Says nothing but continues to handle the plant and look at her watch*]

Therapist: I feel I must set a limit that you cannot touch this plant. I'll have to change seats with you so you can't reach it.

Jan: [*Stops touching the plant but continues to ignore the therapist*]

Therapist: I'm getting a very definite feeling that you're angry at me.

Jan: [*Says nothing*]

Therapist: I'm feeling more strongly all the time that you're angry, but that you can't come right out and say so.

Jan: [*Remains silent*]

Therapist: I also feel welling up within me a hope that some day you'll be comfortable enough to speak right out to me about your anger.

Jan: You wouldn't like that.

Therapist: I know it's hard for you to believe that I could handle it, but *I* feel I'd like the opportunity to try.

Jan: Well, I can do it.

Therapist: I don't understand why you don't then.

Jan: Okay, I'm mad at you because I have to think of something "psychological" to talk about every time I come in here and sometimes I can't think of anything.

Therapist: [*Changing from congruence to empathy*] You feel like I'm making demands, and that makes you angry.

Jan: Yeah, and I thought if I messed with the plant enough, you'd kick me out and the session would be over.

Therapist: So maybe you're angry with me for keeping you here.

Jan: Well, I was, but not so much now.

Letting the child know (congruently) that she is irritating provides sound and possibly useful information. Doing so in a nonrejecting manner keeps the statement from lowering either the client's self-esteem or the quality of therapist-client relationship. Dealing congruently with what is experienced by the client and therapist precludes any game playing and manipulation by the client, and it models congruent functioning in the process.

Not Buying

Another way in which congruence can be effective is in a technique called "not buying." The child may tell the therapist something the therapist does not believe or agree with. Leaving the assertion unchallenged would be destructive to the child. So, in this example, this therapist, respecting the child's right to believe whatever he wishes, retains the same right for himself and disagrees.

Tommy: Those IQ tests are too hard for me. I'm really stupid.

Therapist: I can understand how you feel, and that's okay but I have a different opinion. Just for the record, I don't think you're dumb. I've been with you awhile, and I've seen you perform. To me you seem like a very intelligent child.

Tommy: You really think so?

Therapist: I really think so.

Or the child may misinterpret the therapist's thoughts or motivations; this is an excellent opportunity to model congruence by "not buying."

Tommy: Can we go for a walk today?

Therapist: Well, the first few times we went for a walk, I thought that was a good idea. Our relationship seemed to grow closer, but now the outdoors seems to distract you from focusing on your strongest feelings. I respect your right either to talk about your feelings or not to talk about them, but I don't think I should agree to move our therapy to a location which I feel may *hamper* consideration of feelings.

Tommy: You're mad at me, aren't you?

Therapist: No.

Tommy: You don't like me. You don't even care. I bet you like all your other patients better than you like me. If one of your patients asked you to take him for a walk, I bet you wouldn't say no.

Therapist: I understand that right now you feel I don't like you and that's okay. But I know I *do* like you.

Tommy: What do you mean?

Therapist: I know I *do* like you. It's okay for you to think I don't, but it's got to be all right for me to know that I do. I refuse to buy the idea that I don't like you.

Tommy: Well, you don't. If you weren't so lazy, you'd take me for a walk.

Therapist: So you think it's because I'm lazy.

Tommy: Yeah.

Therapist: Well, if I weren't taking you because I'm lazy, then I really wouldn't care very much about you. But that's not the reason I'm refusing to go. I don't buy that either.

Tommy: What is the reason?

Therapist: Because I feel I should help you deal with your thoughts and feelings, like we're doing right now.

Tommy: This is a lot harder than going for a walk.

Therapist: Yeah, and you'd still like to go for one, wouldn't you?

Tommy: Yeah.

Therapist: Part of me is sorry that I can't agree to go.

Tommy: So, let's play a game of checkers.

Therapist: You feel like that'd be the next best thing to a walk?

Tommy: Yeah, and I'm really gonna beat you today. I feel lucky.

The congruent therapist's feelings are available to him and are at the service of the client. Rogers (1975b) expressed it this way:

Congruence clearly involves self-awareness, meaning that not only are the therapist's feelings and experiences available to himself but that he is able to live and be these feelings in the relationship. It means that this is a direct personal encounter with the client, a meeting with him on a person-to-person basis. It means that the therapist is *being* himself, not denying himself. (p. 1835)

Transference

The concept of transference does not refer only to sexual feelings or those displaced from parents onto the therapist. Any time an individual imposes something on a relationship or interaction that the relationship does not justify, he or she is displacing or transferring emotions. Transference is an inappropriate generalization resulting from expectations based on previous experience. Such transference can be among the most valuable therapeutic data because it reveals the child's pathology. The therapist using it relies not on the client's recollections, but on concrete examples of behavior which occur before the eyes of both the client and the therapist.

The concept of transference is extremely important in Freudian psychoanalysis and in most other dynamically oriented approaches. It has not heretofore been a component of Rogerian psychotherapy. However, therapists who place a strong emphasis on congruence must acknowledge that when an incident involving transference occurs in therapy, the skilled therapist will be alerted by the experience and will endeavor to take advantage of it. Being congruent, he or she will not let thoughts about such a relevant event go unexpressed. Thus, through heavy reliance on congruence, an opening is provided which allows a limited reliance on transference techniques.

Carol: I've been reading this novel about a teenage girl who's an alcoholic.
Therapist: You sound like you find it really interesting.
Carol: Yeah, it's a good book—real to life.
Therapist: Like in real life where young people experiment with alcohol or other drugs.
Carol: [*Sits up straight quickly with a startled reaction*] What do you mean by that?
Therapist: Wow, I must have touched a tender nerve.
Carol: What do you mean? What're you getting at? What're you saying?
Therapist: Well, I really wasn't saying anything except understanding the fact that you were reading a book which seemed real to you. But *now* I'm beginning to feel something *else,* and that is that you feel like I'm accusing you of something.

Carol: Aren't you?

Therapist: No, but you seem to feel like I'm snooping to see if I can catch you.

Carol: Yeah, that's how it feels.

Therapist: That's very interesting because it gives me a feeling that, as a therapist, I can't avoid.

Carol: What's that?

Therapist: It's the feeling that you are misunderstanding me and distorting what I'm saying.

Carol: I don't understand.

Therapist: My word for it is transference. It simply means that if people in your past, possibly parents, or people in the present, such as your house-mother or teachers, ask you a question, maybe some of them *are* trying to pin something on you or one of your friends. But I'm not, *I* know that. So what may be going on is that you see everyone as questioning and snooping when they may just be interested in you. I'm troubled that it may not be easy for you to have a close and trusting relationship, particularly with an adult, because sooner or later you will perceive them as being out to get you even if they're not. If this is true, it's bound to impair what would otherwise be rewarding relationships with a lot of people.

Carol: Are you mad at me? You've never talked to me before like this. You seem to be putting me down, but on the other hand you don't *seem* to be mad at me.

Therapist: No, I'm not mad, but I *am* talking very straight to you.

Carol: What's bothering you is that you feel like I accused you of prying when you weren't.

Therapist: The fact that you misjudged me doesn't hurt my feelings, but your tendency to do that makes me concerned that it might hurt your relationships with other people.

Carol: I think I see what you're getting at, but this is really heavy. Its difficult—hard to understand.

Therapist: Maybe you'd like to think about it, and if you want we can talk about it some more at a later time.

Carol: Okay.

Therapist: And if you're willing, I'd like to keep bringing these things up and pointing them out if I think they're happening.

Carol: That's okay.

Therapist: Like a while ago, you almost did it again and then caught yourself.

Carol: How's that?

Therapist: You seemed on the verge of jumping to the conclusion that I was mad when I wasn't. But you caught yourself right in the middle of it.

Carol: Yeah!

Therapist: So maybe you have a tendency to read anger into relationships when it isn't there.

Later the client began referring to her tendency to transfer inappropriate perceptions into other relationships, and she seemed to be making progress in perceiving others more objectively. She frequently cited this conversation as the beginning of such awareness.

The younger the child, the more difficult it will be to explain transference and to use it. Such use is possible and valuable, but the younger the child, the simpler the explanation must be. The following example illustrates how transference can be explored with a younger child. Pam is a 6-year-old with a history of having been punished if her mother thought she was having angry or sexually related thoughts. In the early stages of therapy she was inhibited, and she avoided expressing angry feelings.

Therapist: You seem upset because I didn't bring the finger paints.
Pam: It's okay.
Therapist: You *say* it's okay but you act like you're put out.
Pam: I *am not!* You can't say I'm angry.
Therapist: You seem to feel that I would get after you if you were angry, but around me it's okay to feel angry. Maybe sometime soon you will decide that it's okay to feel angry or upset around some people.

Resolving Apparent Contradictions

Is the use of transference such as that cited above a violation of the principle of responsibility? The therapist may seem to be taking over for the client by becoming didactic. But whether there is such a violation depends on how the material is offered. The use of transference must be consistent with the phenomenologic position of "this is how *I* see it, and not necessarily how it *is*." More importantly, the material must be offered on a take-it-or-leave-it basis, not imposed upon the client. Although some minimal violation of the principle of responsibility may be unavoidable, the therapist's denying or failing to disclose perception of a transference phenomenon and those feelings associated with such a perception might constitute a greater violation of an equally important principle—congruence. In the post-Wisconsin era, the emphasis is clearly on congruence, but with minimal infringement in the area of responsibility.

If a child makes us really angry and we say so, are we not contradicting the principle of unconditional positive regard? The answer should be no. Feeling such regard for someone who never irritates us is not difficult; but accepting

someone who makes us angry is truly unconditional positive regard. Expressing that anger with acceptance communicates not only unconditional positive
regard but also congruence. Gendlin (1974, 1981, 1986) explained in this way:

> You will notice that I have been saying what the therapist ought to do, all in one
> principle: Maximizing the client's experiential process, using our own to do so. But
> this can be said specifically in terms of the three "conditions" which phrased it in
> more old-fashioned language. *Empathy* seemed to be restating the client's verbal
> content, although really it always meant pointing sensitively to his felt meaning to
> help him focus on it and carry it further. *Congruence* seemed to mean saying what we
> as therapists thought. Really it meant responding from out of our own ongoing
> experiential process, showing the steps of thought and feeling we go through,
> responding not stiltedly or artifically, but out of our felt being. As verbal content,
> congruence seems contradictory to empathy (in empathy we tell only exactly about
> the client, while in congruence we tell about ourselves). As experiential processes,
> empathy and congruence are exactly the same thing, the direct expression of what
> we are now going through with the client, in response to him. Finally, *unconditional*
> *positive regard* as content contradicts the other two. "If you don't like him now, then
> you aren't unconditional, and if you say so, you're not empathic, but if you keep still
> about it, you're incongruent." But unconditional regard really meant appreciating
> the client as a person regardless of not liking what he is up against in himself
> (responding to him in his always positive struggle against whatever he is trapped in).
> It includes our expressions of dismay and even anger, but always in the context of
> both of us knowing we are seeking to meet each other warmly and honestly as
> people, exactly at the point at which each are and feel. Both are highly formal
> denials of a real relationship. One role-played a perfectly neutral acceptance. We see
> two of a kind—artificial, formalistic avoidances of genuine interaction between two
> people. The patient's real feelings were also considered invalid (transference). The
> analyst's feelings were also considered invalid (counter-transference). Similarly in
> client-centered therapy, it was a mistake for the therapist to interject his own feelings
> into the therapeutic situation. Today, client-centered therapists make "genuineness"
> the first condition for therapy and therapist-expressivity and spontaneity main
> therapeutic factors. Psychoanalysts are also moving toward real involvement and
> commitment as persons, with less reliance on technique. (1974, 549)

A fully functioning therapist, then, uses every technique available to help the
client, beginning with congruence. If properly conveyed, this will not be in
conflict with valuing. It will be done *because* the therapist values the client.

Valuing

To the extent that the therapist finds himself experiencing a warm acceptance of each aspect of the

A third good condition for growth is continuous and unconditional valuing.
The condition has been called *prizing* by John Dewey, *loving* by others, and
unconditional positive regard by Rogers and most of the client-centered group. We
choose the term *valuing* because it is a direct description with very little distortion and because the others tend to sound a bit contrived in today's usage.
Considerable research (Truax and Carkhuff 1964) has shown that valuing is
important to therapeutic progress with adults. One study (Truax et al. 1973)
confirms this finding with children. According to Rogers's (1957) theory of
personality, feelings about self come from "evaluational interactions with others"; so that every time a person interacts with someone else, an assessment
process transpires. A person cannot have another human being come into his or
her perceptual field without some evaluational process occurring; therefore, all
interactions are to some extent evaluational.

The Importance of Valuing

Of course, certain interactions are more significant than others. The more
significant the other person to the maintenance and enhancement of the self, the
more weight the interaction will have. In an important formative period such as
the early years of life, highly significant others, namely parents, play key roles
in forming the child's positive or negative concepts about self. As the child
matures, other people also play important roles, not necessarily of the same
magnitude. If the therapist is successful in establishing an intimate relationship
with the child, he or she will become a "highly significant other" in the eyes of
the child, and what the therapist does then becomes very important. This is the
situation that Strupp (1973) referred to as the "power base from which the
therapist influences the patient." In his psychoanalytic framework, this is understood in terms of enhanced transference. But the important point is that if the
therapist values the child significantly and with congruence, this unique experience will enhance the possibility of the child's valuing him or herself. If the
therapist is not unique to the child in such a way that the child perceives the

therapist's valuing as genuine and significant, then the relationship may not yet be adequate to promote growth.

The most basic tenet of self-concept theory is that the way in which a person thinks and feels about him or herself is the most important determinant of behavior. Behaviorists believe that learning plays the key role in determining behavior. Self-concept theorists retort that if this is so, it is how we have learned to perceive ourselves (positively or negatively) that is critical.

Many psychoanalytic theorists suggest that an ability to *ex*press rather than *re*press thoughts and feelings is the critical determinant of behavior. But many theorists within the analytic tradition, including Sullivan (1947), acknowledge the importance of self-concept. To the phenomenologic theorist, it is the single most important factor.

These theoretical statements imply some assumptions; for instance, they assume that clients tend to feel unwanted and unworthy. This feeling will vary among children, but as a rule all psychotherapy clients either consciously or unconsciously do feel unwanted and unworthy. The correlation is quite high between the degree of psychopathology and the degree of self-depreciation, rejection of self, and lack of self-esteem.

There are at least two views regarding the origins of individual self-concept. We have already mentioned Rogers's idea that it comes from so-called evaluational interactions with others. Sullivan (1947) hypothesized that these basic feelings about self crystallize much earlier. He stressed the importance of the mother–child relationship during infancy, saying that the affective impact of the child on significant others (e.g., the mother) is most critical. For instance, if a baby with colic has trouble nursing and cries often, the mother may feel inadequate and frustrated, and the infant may sense her feelings. The mother then relates to the infant in a manner that meets the infant's needs even less. This supposedly accelerates the cycle of negative self-concept, negative impact on others, and negative response from others, which in turn reinforces the negative self-concept.

The views of Sullivan and Rogers are not necessarily incompatible. The Sullivanian notion may explain the child's earliest feelings toward self or the factors that predispose one toward either a positive or negative self-concept. Rogers's ideas explain what happens after the child becomes capable of developing a concept of self and an understanding of such abstract concepts as acceptance and rejection.

Unconditional Valuing

The term *unconditional* is important to the concept of valuing; it means continuous in time. The valuing never lapses and does not depend on the responses of the client. In the life of the child, being cared about may be conditional upon such things as bringing home a good report card, not being angry at little brother, or eating all one's dinner. Unconditional valuing by the therapist is likely to be a new experience. Whether or not the therapist had a fight with her husband, the therapist values the child; whether she's feeling well or poorly, whether she's had a good day or not, the valuing is consistent. The child is valued by the therapist irrespective of whether the child values the therapist. The child is valued equally, whether he or she pleases or angers the therapist, or even if he or she implies that the therapist is incompetent.

Unconditional valuing does not mean that therapists enjoy everything their clients do, or even that they like the clients in the traditional sense of the word; people can have unconditional positive regard for their enemies. The concept is a philosophic commitment involving the capacity to recognize and acknowledge in every human being a humanness that is automatically worthy of appreciation and valuing. The personality of therapists, however, must be such that they can respond effectively and interpersonally to this basic human worth in all clients.

In some ways, however, the word *unconditional* is not what it suggests. For instance, unconditional does not mean that there are no degrees, but that the difference in degree should depend more on the therapist's philosophic commitment, experience, and maturity than it does on the moment-to-moment aspects of the therapeutic interactions.

Carrie, an 11-year-old with school phobia, did not want to come for her therapy hour, and when she arrived, was unwilling to work. She slouched in her chair, rapped her fingers on the wooden arm, and looked out the window. She would neither speak nor respond to the therapist.

> *Therapist:* I find myself wishing you'd communicate with me directly, even just to say you're angry.
> *Carrie:* [No response]
> *Therapist:* I feel for you when I see you so sullen. It's up to you, whether or not you talk, but I want you to know that I am concerned.
> *Carrie:* [No response]
> *Therapist:* [Congruently] And I'm not going to give up. I'm going to stick with you until you're over your problem. I care too much to give up, even when you seem to be telling me that you'd like for both of us to give in.

The therapist was frustrated by Carrie's sullen refusal to work, but was able to say so in a way that reaffirmed the fact that he valued her. By letting her know that he was committed to working with her despite this setback, he was saying that he valued her enough to stay even though it was occasionally unpleasant. This valuing did not keep him from letting her know how her behavior affected him, but he was talking out his feelings, not acting them out. His tone of voice was calm and matter-of-fact, describing his reactions without condemnation.

Unconditional valuing is important for children of all ages. Troy, a 3-year-old, was having difficulty in adjusting following the birth of his new baby brother, Lynn. He reportedly whined or cried continually, clung to his mother, and stubbornly asked to sleep in the new baby's crib. Troy's parents sought help from a child therapist, since it seemed to them that the disorder was not only serious, but on the verge of becoming chronic. Also, both parents had become concerned about the rage Troy's behavior had ellicited from the father. Punishment had become overly zealous on several occasions, leaving Troy with telltale red welts on his buttocks and legs.

The therapist decided to model his instuctions to the parents about how to value Troy unconditionally during these difficult times. Troy, his parents, and his 6-week-old brother all came for a session. Troy began to whine and cling early in the meeting. The mother displayed agitation but allowed Troy to fuss and hold on.

Father: See what I mean. It's like this all the time. Now settle down, Troy! Quit whinning and leave your mother alone. Why do you let him do that, Mary? You're as much to blame as he is.

Mother: Well, what am I supposed to do? You don't have to worry about this because he's afraid of you.

Father: [*To therapist*] Do you think she should just let him do that?

Troy: [*Grabs baby's rattle, scratching the latter's hand in the process with his fingernails and causing the baby to cry*]

Therapist: [*Picks up Troy lovingly and retrieves rattle from his hand*] I love you just as much as Lynn, so I want to be sure you have something to play with, too. [*Then, pulling a box of toys from a closet*] Here, Troy, you choose one you like. [*The therapist continues to hold Troy lovingly*]

Troy: [*Chooses a block to play with*]

Therapist: [*Continues to hold Troy and returns the rattle to Lynn*]

Troy: [*Remains quiet and interacts by placing block gently against the therapist's nose*]

The therapist's modeling of unconditional valuing to Troy's parents was a critical ingredient of therapy with this family. Troy's parents began to provide him with some extra support and caring. They also learned to convey valuing or caring to him at difficult moments. With these changes Troy was than able to adjust to the addition of a new sibling at home.

Apparent Contradictions between Congruence and Valuing

In therapy there are times when negative affect must be expressed congruently, when limits must be set, and when the child must be given the data about the negative affect his or her actions create, but without rejection. The therapist must be able to convey verbally the message of negative affect without acting it out, even through tone of voice or facial expression.

Some would say that a therapist calmly telling a child he or she is angry is being incongruent, but that is not so. Such a response would be adaptive and well-conceived by the therapist who realizes the benefits of acknowledging and sharing true feelings without judging the person who generated those feelings, even when the affect is negative.

Testing Unconditional Valuing

Children are, for the same reason that they need therapy, likely to be difficult to convince that they are valued. In fact, when they begin to get an inkling of it, they may purposely become most difficult to value in order to test whether the unconditional valuing is truly unconditional. "Well," the child thinks, "he says he likes me even when I spill the paint, let's see if he likes me when I throw it on the wall." Children who feel worthless will act in a manner congruent with their perception of self. Being valued and feeling valued then creates dissonance (i.e. Festinger 1957). Misbehaving is a way both of resolving dissonance and of having the guarantee of valuing before risking the vulnerability inherent in discarding defenses against rejection.

Every individual is entitled to love and esteem from significant others. Most of those who find themselves in therapy are children who were deprived of such a human response or who somehow misinterpreted it. The question then becomes: How does the therapist fulfill such a need?

Conveying Unconditional Regard

The first step in conveying unconditional regard is to realize that valuing is not so much a technique as an attitude or an emotion. These are not things a congruent therapist can turn on and off with a switch. If they are present, they will be felt, but some deliberate effort can help to highlight the fact that the client is valued.

It is important to show interest in the child, to express that interest nonverbally, and to let the child *experience* it as opposed to being told about it. The therapist becomes important by focusing, by being willing to go wherever the child wants to go in both the dialogue and the relationship. Such valuing is communicated from the first contact.

> *Therapist:* [*Encountering the client in waiting room*] Hello, Joey, I'm Dr. Weaver. [*Therapist extends his hand and smiles*]
> *Joey:* Hi. [*Shakes hands*]
> *Therapist:* I'm very happy to meet you; I've been anxious to get acquainted since Dr. Young told me you were coming.
> *Joey:* [*Smiles nervously*]
> *Therapist:* Will you come with me this way to my office? [*Gestures toward far door and Joey accompanies him down the hallway*]
> *Therapist:* [*Opening door for Joey and guiding him in with a firm, warm hand on the shoulder*] This is my office. Will you sit down?
> *Joey:* Thanks.

Both Joey and the therapist are seated. The therapist leans toward the client and smiles, communicating warmth and interest as well as acceptance.

This therapist has used these first few minutes to convey his unconditional valuing to Joey by his positive warm response, his tone of voice, and his posture, by opening the door for the child and letting him go through first, and by putting a hand on his shoulder.

Another way of valuing is simply making verbal statements. What the child hears and what he or she experiences may differ; the experience is always more important than what the child hears. It will not be adequate, then, for the therapist simply to tell the client that he or she is valued or good, but there is a place for this sort of valuing if it is both reality-based and congruent with what the child *experiences* from the therapist. If it is not based on reality, it will be incongruent, ineffectual, and possibly detrimental.

Statements such as, "I like you a lot Michael; I look forward to seeing you each week, and what happens to you has become terribly important to me, too," have their place, as do less profound utterances such as, "You're such a creative child, it's amazing sometimes what you can come up with," or even, "Your hair is very pretty today."

Making valuing statements when the child is not doing something pleasing to the therapist makes sense from the standpoint of self-concept theory, as does avoiding valuing statements when a child is trying to please. This procedure also makes sense to learning theorists. Therapists do not try to condition clients to behave in certain ways under certain conditions; they try to change the child's basic feelings about self. Once these are changed, behavior will be different under all conditions. So the ideal time to make valuing statements to children is when they are not doing anything particularly pleasing. Then the statements indicate that they are worthy individuals apart from their acts. They are valued all of the time for what they are, not just for what they do to please others. Children's attempts to please others result in conditional self-esteem and an external locus of evaluation and control. This tends to make children "other-directed" rather than "inner-directed." Therapists must not foster the pathologic condition wherein children feel worthy only if they please others and unworthy when they do not, lest they develop into driven people who are continually trying to please others, seldom succeeding, remaining unhappy and unfulfilled.

Comments such as, "I enjoy you," "I'm comfortable with you," can be beneficial. Sometimes being with the client in his or her negative feelings shows that the therapist cares: "It hurts me to know that you're feeling so friendless at school." Sometimes the therapist is the one who inadvertently hurts the child; but such an incident can still be used as a time to value the child and create a therapeutic moment.

> *Therapist:* [*Near end of session*] I won't be able to see you next week. I'm going to be out of town and we won't be able to meet.
> *Will:* [*Looking disappointed*] Oh.
> *Therapist:* I'm going to miss you and our time together.
> *Will:* [*Softly*] I'll miss you, too.
> *Therapist:* And you're going to be out of school for vacation.
> *Will:* Yeah! I'll get out of school.
> *Therapist:* I hope it's fun, and I'll look forward to seeing you in two weeks.

Giving and Receiving Gifts

At times valuing can be conveyed appropriately in experiential psychotherapy by giving and receiving gifts. This is in contrast to the rules of some other approaches to working with children. Some therapists may interpret the symbolism of gifts and may adhere to stringent rules regarding them, while others may prohibit gift-giving lest it disrupt the treatment process. However, to the experiential therapist, the appropriateness of a gift is assessed within the context of its effect on the therapeutic relationship.

Offering a gift may affirm intimacy. Some children share presents with therapists as a way of demonstrating caring or valuing. Typically these are creations or drawings made by them. Acceptance of such gifts can facilitate the therapy process, and failure to accept them might impair rapport or relationship. Sometimes, however, children give for other reasons. For example, a child may give presents compulsively in order to be accepted or liked. In such instances the therapist might congruently acknowledge a present but reassure the child that he or she is liked or valued for him or herself.

At times, experiential therapists may also wish to give a gift to a child client. Experiential therapists may give gifts sparingly for special moments or occasions. Holidays, graduation, birthdays, or termination may, for example, sometimes call for a small present. Therapists, of course, should not give gifts in an attempt to develop an intimate therapeutic relationship—intimacy needs to be developed in other ways. Similarly, the therapist should not feel compelled to share a present. Again, the appropriateness of giving has to be assessed in terms of its effects on the relationship.

Non-possessive Warmth

Hobbs (1962) makes an analogy that the therapeutic relationship is best compared to falling in love. This is rich with meaning and is probably as good a prototype as any to explain exactly what is meant by unconditional valuing. In therapy with children, the love resembles the love between parent and child. The therapist is, in fact, modeling selfless and nonpossessive love in this relationship.

Valuing is fostered by all of the other good conditions for therapy. It is fostered by locus of responsibility when the therapist allows the client to direct the therapy, saying, in effect, "I respect you as a person, and I respect your right to be quiet if you want to be quiet, to talk if you want to talk; I respect your right to choose what you will do with our time together and to choose how we use this therapeutic opportunity." Focusing the locus of responsibility in the child says, "I have confidence in you and in your ability to choose for yourself, and confidence that you'll come out all right if left to yourself."

Relating to a child with intimacy, with congruence, and with empathy tells the child that he or she is valued. The good conditions are so entwined that dividing them can be misleading. They are not five different puzzle pieces which, when put together properly, make a whole called experiential therapy. Rather, they are more like five ingredients of a recipe which, stirred together, blend so that one is indistinguishable from another.

Empathy

> This formulation would state that it is the counselor's function to assume insofar as he is able, the internal frame of reference of the client, to perceive the world as the client sees it, to perceive the client himself as he is seen by himself, to lay aside

Empathy can be defined as understanding, but it is a special, and for the most part, elusive kind of understanding which many people do not comprehend. Empathic understanding is not a style of interaction to which most people are accustomed—mild distortion, misunderstanding, and evaluation are more common. Thus, initially, empathy feels somewhat unnatural for most students of psychotherapy.

The usual form of understanding is what might be called "diagnostic understanding"; this form attempts to understand *why*. Why does Suzie behave so badly with her little brother? What makes Bill throw tantrums about going to school? Many psychotherapists are so interested in insight that they become caught up in diagnostic endeavors, leaving no energies for empathy. Empathy does not concern itself with the "why's" of Suzie's behavior, but focuses on her feelings and on what she is experiencing from *her* point of view. This may require an understanding (and acceptance) of the fact that she does not like her brother, at least at the moment; or possibly that he simply annoys her. Empathy must be without evaluation ("That's bad; you shouldn't hate your brother") and without interpretation ("You're cross because you missed your nap"). Rogers (1975a) wrote:

> The way of being with another person which is termed empathic has several facets. It means entering the private perceptual world of the other and becoming thoroughly at home in it. It involves being sensitive, moment to moment, to the changing felt meanings which flow in this other person, to the fear or rage or tenderness or confusion or whatever, that he/she is experiencing. It means temporarily living in his/her life, moving about in it delicately without making judgments, sending meanings of which he/she is scarcely aware, but not trying to uncover feelings of which the person is totally unaware, since this would be too threatening. It includes communicating your sensings of his/her world as you look with fresh and unfrightened eyes at elements of which the individual is fearful. It means frequently checking with him/her as to the accuracy of your sensings, and being guided by the responses you receive. You are a confident companion to the person in his/her inner world. By pointing to the possible meanings in the flow of his/her experiencing, you help the person to focus on this useful type of reference, to experience the meanings more fully, and to move forward in the experiencing.
>
> To be with another in this way means that for the time being you lay aside the

views and values you hold for yourself in order to enter another's world without prejudice. In some sense it means that you lay aside yourself and this can only be done by a person who is secure enough in himself that he knows he will not get lost in what may turn out to be the strange or bizarre world of the other, and can comfortably return to his own world when he wishes.

Perhaps this description makes clear that being empathic is a complex, demanding, strong yet subtle and gentle way of being. (p. 4)

The Difference between Empathy and Sympathy

Empathic understanding can be differentiated from sympathy. For our purposes, we will define sympathy as experiencing affectively what another individual is experiencing. If the therapist responds to depression by becoming depressed, that is sympathy. If, however, the therapist understands the client's depression from the client's point of view without duplicating it internally, he or she is being empathic. The better the therapist cognitively understands the uniqueness of the child's depression and the way that depression feels in a given moment, the more empathic he or she is.

The ideal therapeutic response is empathy accompanied by genuine and sensitive feelings belonging only to the therapist, free of sympathy. Therapists' empathic understanding may be obscured if they sympathize. Having the same feelings, or what seem to be the same feelings, that the child has can absorb or divert therapists' energies. Therapists may focus on their own phenomenologic field and inappropriately project feelings on the other individual, or they may be so smitten with feelings that the concentration or focusing necessary to grasp the uniqueness of *another's* experience is lost. For example, if a physician is attempting to be supportive of the parents of a child who has died, and is experiencing the grief, anger, hurt, and frustration of those parents, the physician may be unable to help them. But if that therapist can remain reasonably free from the parents' feelings, can avoid participating in their grief but at the same time maintain concern and sensitivity, and can be cognitively and intellectually aware in a way that grasps the fullness of their grief, then he or she is in an optimal position, both emotionally and perceptually, to be of help.

Knowing How to Listen

In order to have something to listen to, the therapist must first develop the capacity to keep quiet and otherwise facilitate the child's self-expression. Thus, the locus of responsibility for conversation and its content must be clearly vested in the child. This is often accomplished more by what therapists do *not* do (such as talking) than by what they do (empathizing, valuing).

Contrary to some stereotypes, neo-Rogerian therapists are quite active, typically intervening frequently but briefly; they are neither as passive as Freudian analysts in the early sessions nor as wordy as typical directive therapists, but they must be quiet internally so as to be able to focus on the child. Even when there are no verbal cues from the client, there will be nonverbal ones to listen for and perceive. If therapists are thinking about what they are going to do during the next hour, or worrying about an unfinished task, their ability to empathize will be hampered. The facility for total concentration does not come easily, and once acquired, is maintained with effort.

Good listening involves being able to free oneself from one's own frame of reference and focus on the child's frame of reference. Some listeners are always reminded of similar experiences they have had and can hardly wait to relate them. This, of course, is not empathy, or even good listening, because the listener is not hearing the speaker but is only responding to self through another's voice.

Empathic Responses to Nonverbal Material

Skilled child therapists cannot limit their empathic response to childrens' words alone; the overwhelming majority of the cues from children are nonverbal. They must listen to the silences and know whether a silence is deliberate or simply awkward. They must sense their clients' feelings and verbalize this understanding. This not only enables them to function as empathic helpers but can also help the children to come into better contact with feelings about which they are only minimally aware. More opportunities for congruence are thus opened up via the modeling of self-awareness and self-disclosure. Verbalizing feelings also serves as a model for the children's own communication and thus for their level of adjustment, teaching them not to become enslaved by words but to respond to and to sense whatever messages the therapist is sending. For example, it might help them to avoid mistaking an angry, but sullen, person for someone who is not angry at all.

Empathy Is Not Agreement

Some adults, including psychotherapists, are often reluctant to give empathic responses to certain potentially maladaptive statements made by children or adolescents, lest these be misinterpreted as agreement. Perhaps the child will imagine that the aberrant behavior that is known, but not condemned, is being condoned. Empathy is, however, neither agreement nor disagreement, although the child may misinterpret it initially as agreement or approval. A girl may tell the therapist that she is furious with Father; the therapist will accept that anger and accept the child who has that anger, with no argument or chaffing. The girl may see this acceptance as the therapist's siding against her father, but with time and with the development of intimacy, she will come to understand that this is not so. Probably no harm will come from the child's believing temporarily that the therapist is agreeing. It may be counter-therapeutic for the therapist to structure therapy by explaining this or to state in the early stages of therapy that he or she is empathizing but not necessarily agreeing with the child.

Neither does empathy conflict with the therapist's congruence or possession of personal convictions. The therapist has personal values but is still able to understand the child's point of view. Such behavior may, in fact, serve as a valuable model for the child.

Focusing on Feeling rather than Content

The novice therapist, in initial attempts to understand or communicate with a child, will often become embroiled in the content of that child's words. Suppose a teenager says, "I'm so upset. I don't know whether I should transfer to another school or stay where I am." To help that individual, it is not necessary to talk about school. One does, however, have to discuss such mental states as ambivalence and confusion, and the affect that accompanies them, i.e., anxiety, depression, or anger. Notice how in the following example the client dwells on content (a storm) but the therapist confines himself to a discussion of feeling.

> *Sean:* [*A 9-year-old with serious kidney disease that may be terminal*] Did the hail storm hit your house?
> *Therapist:* No, I was lucky.
> *Sean:* It hit our house while my dad was fishing, and one of my puppies got out in the storm and it died.
> *Therapist:* That made you feel very sad.
> *Sean:* Yeah, and my cousin and I were at the house and we heard the storm and jumped up, but it was already there.
> *Therapist:* It was scary.
> *Sean:* Yeah!
> *Therapist:* Those scary memories tend to stay on your mind and don't go away.

Sean: Yeah, how did you know?

Therapist: I guess because you bring things like that up and we talk about them a lot.

Sean: Oh.

Therapist: And it's probably not just the scary thoughts that remain, but the scary feelings hang on, too.

A boy may be talking about whether or not his parents treated him properly when they burned his comic books, or made him sell his dog, or gave him a spanking. For him, the focus is on the content ("My books are burned!"); he is full of feelings, and that is likely the very reason he cannot focus on them. But for the therapist, the issue is affect, the feelings of the child at a given moment as they relate to the content he is discussing.

Nondirective therapy has been criticized for being *too* directive (Robinson 1950) with its dogged insistence on focusing on the feelings of the client. The therapist is saying, in effect, "You can talk about whatever you want, but I'm going to concentrate on your feelings." In this sense, nondirective therapy really is directive.

Empathy Must Be Communicated

Communicating empathic feelings is as important as having them. The child may grasp some sense of the therapist's empathy, but explicit communication is the best way of assuring that it is felt. This is not easy; it requires skill to communicate empathy and to have it be understood for what it is.

Reflection is one technique for conveying empathy. This usually involves a summary statement made periodically by the therapist. It must be in the therapist's own words, and should, of course, focus on the child's feelings. Rather than echoing or parroting the content of what the child says, the reflection relies on brief summary statements of feelings expressed, such as "You feel disliked by your classmates," or, "You're still angry with your parents, aren't you?" If the therapist has grasped the child's feeling in its fullness, a simple reflective statement will convey this fact.

Sometimes, however, the therapist cannot be certain about the child's feelings, and the achievement of empathy then becomes more of a struggle. The therapist must abandon reflection in favor of an empathic question: "Is this what you mean?" or "Do I understand you correctly that . . . ?" Such questions are *not* probes. Probing questions ask the child to talk about something he or she is not already talking about or trying to talk about. Take the adolescent who says, "I don't know whether to transfer from this school to another." A reflective question or a question in the service of empathy could take many forms, such as, "Is there some part of you that wants to go in one direction and another part of you that wants to go in another?" or "Is there some part of you that wants to please yourself yet another part that wants to please someone else?" These questions would be in the service of empathy. A probe, however, would take a different form, such as "Well, have you ever thought about whether you might lose some credits if you were to transfer?" This is what helpers often do when they lack genuine skills or the ability to create good therapeutic conditions. Probing questions are common crutches for the inept helper.

Sometimes the child will give the therapist very little, if anything, to reflect. Just when the helper is willing and available to be totally empathic, a girl comes to therapy wanting to talk about Bambi. Children have a way of taking an hour and a half to talk about an hour-and-a-half-long movie, limiting the value of the 50-minute therapy session. The temptation is to try to get her off the subject of Bambi and onto something with more feeling content, something more psychologically minded. But she may be avoiding that or may, indeed, have found Bambi more exciting than anything she could think of to share with the therapist. Perhaps in relating the story the girl is trying to be kind, believing the therapist will enjoy it as much as she did. But from some therapists' points of view, children who do this are throwing them crumbs rather than giving them a loaf. The temptation is to confront them and demand that they focus instead on something more appropriate to the therapy hour.

Skilled experiential therapists will make no such demands; instead they will take the crumbs and savor them, and will convey this savoring through empathy and valuing. Demanding more would likely create defensiveness. Therapists should do the best work possible with the crumbs, understanding as well as they can and trying to make it as safe and pleasurable as possible for their clients to have expressed a little bit of feeling, in whatever confusing, mystifying, evasive way they have been able to express it. Therapists have to dig in and work with the thrown crumbs. If there was some aspect of the movie that aroused feelings of excitement or fear, the therapist might say, "Sounds like you really had fun. It's nice to do something you really enjoy," or, "That forest fire seems to have reminded you of times when you felt helpless, like a little animal in a world that was on fire and about to overtake it." There may not be much to go on, but the therapist has to take a stab at it, constantly looking for affect. The child can talk about Bambi all she wants, but the therapist will be sure to talk about affect. Therapists cannot slip into a shallow or superficial buddylike conversation and relationship. Clients can talk about whatever they choose— that is their right—but therapists will talk about affect in as great a depth as the client's expressions and capacity for self-awareness will allow. Therapists do the best they can with what they get, never disparaging or ignoring the crumbs and never asking outright for a loaf. If they deserves a loaf, sooner or later they will get it. Whether or not it is deserved depends on how the crumbs are dealt with.

Depth of Empathy

In the early days of client-centered therapy, empathic responses tended to be rather shallow, sometimes reflecting content more than feeling and failing to grasp the client's feelings in all their depth and fullness. In particular, empathic responses did not go beyond the client's immediate awareness. Now, in the neo-Rogerian era, the possibility of facilitating the client's progress beyond that level of immediate awareness is viewed not only as acceptable but as highly desirable.

Empathy can be seen as existing in layers. At the least therapeutic level, the first, the therapist misses the mark completely, and misunderstands what the client is saying:

> *Bob:* I wanted some money for the movies Saturday and Dad wouldn't give me any.
> *Therapist:* You wish you were on your own and didn't have to ask your Dad for money for every little thing?
> *Bob:* No, no. I wish my Mom had been home. She'd have given me some.

The therapist working at the second level of empathy understands content but either misunderstands or ignores feelings.

> *Diane:* All the girls in my class made fun of me because my red dress was above my knees. I didn't think it was too short.
> *Therapist:* The dress was the right length?

At the third level of empathy the therapist focuses on feeling, but lacks appropriate depth:

> *Diane:* The girls in my class teased me because my dress was above my knees.
> *Therapist:* That bothered you a little, right?

The fourth level of empathy involves an understanding of the client's feelings at the level of the client's own awareness.

> *Therapist:* You're really feeling resentful and angry about their teasing, aren't you?

Now, in the neo-Rogerian era, experiential therapists are more likely to go to a fifth level, to take the client further, extending her beyond the level of her current conscious awareness.

> *Therapist: [Sensing from the nonverbal cues a deep feeling of estrangement]* That seems to have made you feel very lonely, like an "outsider."
> *Diane:* Yes, I hadn't thought of that, but I guess you're right.
>
> *or*
>
> *Therapist: [Sensing intense anger of which the child is not immediately aware]* That makes you hate them.
> *Diane:* No, I want to be one of them. *[Pause]* But yes, I do hate them. When they are like that, I want to kill them.

What the therapist did in the fifth-level dialogues was to take the client's unconscious communication, understand it, and bring it to conscious awareness, but the therapist has not taken it so far that the client can not consciously own and confirm the truth of it once she hears it from without rather than from within herself.

The therapist has taken empathy to an improper depth only when the client cannot affirm what the therapist sees and thus has either to dispute the comment or take the therapist's word for it. Then the interaction shifts from empathy to interpretation. This is the precise dividing line between an in-depth empathic response and an interpretation. Dynamic or uncovering therapists often make interpretations, but experiential therapists will never make such statements unless they feel that the client is on the verge of recognizing the feeling and needs only a little encouragement.

Early Rogerian methods suggested that the purpose of empathy was to perform like radar, locating where the client already consciously is. Dynamic psychotherapy has often attempted to perform a kind of instrument landing that is controlled from the ground and designed to get the client on the correct approach and safely landed in the right spot (insight). Neo-Rogerian therapy might be likened to a voice from the control tower which asks the client to check and verify if, in fact, he or she might be slightly off course. The objective is to take the client only to a point of awareness of affect that he or she can genuinely own and affirm, but not beyond. If the client says "No, that's wrong," the therapist agrees, and goes from there. But more mistakes are probably made by therapists who fail to achieve a sufficient level of depth in empathic response than by therapists who go beyond that point, particularly if the latter are willing to retreat when necessary.

Early supportive/relationship therapists felt that therapists had gone beyond empathy when they went beyond a client's current awareness. Experiential therapists know that going beyond current awareness to a point the client genuinely accepts is not beyond empathy; indeed, it is empathy in its fullest, most complete, and possibly most therapeutic form.

The following is an example of a series of in-depth empathic responses that eventually pay off in the form of greater self-awareness in the client.

Therapist: [*In response to nonverbal cues*] You seem very happy today.

Jim: [*A 9-year-old boy with leukemia*] My dad was racing his stock car and the brakes went out.

Therapist: Oh, really? That must have been scary.

Jim: Yeah, his car turned over two times. It went like this [*Speaks loudly and gestures vigorously*]

Therapist: Wow!

Jim: But in the next race he won a trophy.

Therapist: Really?

Jim: He got to go up on a stand in front of the crowd to get his trophy.

Therapist: You were really impressed by that.

Jim: Uh huh. And he went "zoom" and shut his eyes and nearly hit Number 5. Bam!

Therapist: You're impressed by anyone who isn't afraid to meet danger face to face and who comes out on top.

Jim: Uh huh. And Number 3 goes "boom" and Number 5 goes "bam"— he's wiped out every time!

Therapist: Sometimes something that's scary can also be exciting, particularly if it's happening to someone else.

Jim: Yeah, like my cousin had a wreck in a pickup truck and hurt his back.

Therapist: And that was exciting when you heard about it.

Jim: Yeah! He went around the corner and "bam!"

Therapist: But most of the time there's nothing exciting going on and then you just feel bored or depressed.

Jim: Yeah.

Therapist: So sometimes you sit around and dream up exciting things.

Jim: Yeah, it's better than being bored.

Attempts at in-depth (fifth level) empathic responses should not place the therapist in a position of taking the major responsibility for *exploration* (as opposed to identification) of deep feelings. This would violate the principle of locus of responsibility.

Locus of Responsibility

The politics of the client-centered approach is a conscious renunciation and avoidance by the therapist of all control over, or decision-making for, the client. It is the facilitation of self-ownership by the client and the strategies by which this can be achieved; the placing of the locus of decision-making and the responsibility for the effects of these decisions. It is politically centered in the client.

—Rogers, *Carl Rogers on Personal Power*

According to Rogers (1957), the goal of therapy is to move the client away from a state where "his thinking, feeling, and behavior are governed by judgments and expectations of others, and toward a state in which he relies upon his own experience for his values and standards." This is necessary before the child's energies and resourcefulness can be brought to his or her own aid, and before the child can base his or her behavior on direct experience rather than on introjected values.

For many children this is a new and frightening experience, one they would rather not have, particularly if dependency is at the root of some of their difficulty. There may be certain comfort in having parents and teachers make all the value judgments and decisions; being responsible for self may not become appealing until the child has lived with the experience for a while.

In the experiential branch of supportive/relationship psychotherapy, children are not only allowed, but required, to make the important decisions about themselves and about their own behavior. But this concept, in less explicit form, has always influenced client-centered therapy via the therapeutic goal of nonpossessive warmth.

To be consistent with this principle, some therapists must fight a natural tendency to "help" in usurping ways. The experiential therapist resists such impulses, realizing that in order to be truly helpful, one must respect each child's right to self-determination.

Bourne (1974) defines a good parent as one who does not intervene between the child and the consequences of his or her acts. The same may be said of the therapist, since such acts would subvert the learning process.

To be healthy, people must be responsible, but the only way to help children act responsibly is to help them to *feel* responsible. The younger the child, the more difficult it is to implant this concept. For a young child with few verbal skills, an effective way to focus the locus of responsibility in the child is to avoid focusing it elsewhere in the first place. In the playroom, the child may decide to have fun by climbing to a precarious perch on the top of a wheeled toy cart. At such a moment, the therapist must weigh the physical danger involved against the possible setback to relationship that would result (usurpation of locus of responsibility) if he or she took the child off the perch. Is the child in enough danger to warrant the therapist's taking over, or will allowing the child to stay say that the therapist respects the client's right to try new experiences? Such decisions have their limits, of course, and ethical guidelines and legal requirements must be followed. Therapists have to intervene if a client may seriously harm self or others. The therapist must trust his or her "soul's invincible surmise" as to when it would be irresponsible not to intervene.

Thorough respect for the child's personal responsibility should manifest itself in every action of the therapist. For instance, therapists do not decide what is going to happen in therapy, or what is going to be talked about, or even if talk will occur. They neither attempt to ensure progress nor become inappropriately concerned about the speed at which a child is progressing, since the presence of the five optimal conditions will allow the child to grow at his or her maximum rate. Mike's therapy illustrates this point.

Mike is a 6-year-old with a wealth of somatic complaints (e.g., stomach aches, sore throats, etc.) which seemed designed to keep him away from school. In therapy he is quite resistant to choosing an activity. The dialogue that follows is typical of Mike's early sessions.

> *Therapist:* You look like you're waiting for me to tell you what to do.
> *Mike:* [*Nods head in agreement*]
> *Therapist:* Well, I don't think I ought to do that.
> *Mike:* I want you to choose!
> *Therapist:* Well, since I'm not going to, it leaves us with a problem.
> *Mike:* [*Shuffles nervously with hands in pockets*]
> *Therapist:* You seem less happy not playing, but you can't seem to make a choice.
> *Mike:* I want you to do it.
> *Therapist:* I know.
> *Mike:* [*After looking down and remaining silent for 5–7 minutes*] Why don't you choose a game?

Therapist: You'd like to know what I like to do?

Mike: Yes.

Therapist: As long as I'm with you, I'm going to enjoy our time. I like trying to help you in all ways. But I could give you a list of five or six games [*Total of those available in the therapy room*] if that would help you choose.

Mike: Okay.

Therapist: [*Writes available play activities on a sheet of paper, then reads them aloud*]

Mike: I like coloring.

Therapist: [*Produces coloring book and crayons, and the two of them begin to color*]

By refusing to choose an activity, the therapist conveyed that Mike was responsible. The therapist demonstrated that the locus of responsibility must be vested in the client.

Hobbs (pers. comm. June 20, 1961) quoted a therapist who said, "Well, I don't lead my patients, but every once in a while I create a vacuum into which they might be drawn." Such subtle manipulation is inconsistent with a neo-Rogerian approach. If therapist direction is to occur at all, it should come in an aboveboard, congruent fashion, e.g., "I just feel as though a consideration of the consequences might be helpful. Something inside me wants you to look at this issue. But something stronger within me wants you to decide for yourself what you will consider and in what depth."

The Therapist's Values

The issue of whether or not therapists' values should in any way influence psychotherapy has been argued repeatedly. The general feeling among client-centered practitioners was that they should not. There are, however, certain values of therapists which cannot be obscured—they value the health of their clients; they value the clients' expression of positive feelings about self; and they value the clients' right to self-determination. Some studies (e.g., Patterson 1958) have shown that clients tended to misperceive the therapist's moral values, and that they tended to change in the direction of perceived moral values rather than in the direction of actual values.

Sometimes in therapy the child may ask a direct question about the therapist's values, such as "How did you vote in the election?" or "Do you go to church?" Before answering, the therapist must decide what is in the best interests of the child. If relationship is well established, then the child will realize that a therapist's values are but one datum to be considered equally with, but not given more weight than, the values of others. If the child is capable of making judgments based on direct experience, then a direct answer to a question about the therapist's values might be appropriate. If the child is still inclined to introject the therapist's values, then the therapist will probably have to say (congruently) that he or she is afraid his or her values might have an inordinate effect on the child's decision-making, and for that reason would prefer to refrain, at least for the moment, from discussing those values.

Responding to Questions from the Client

There are three general sorts of question with which the therapist must deal. The first type is a statement phrased like a question but requiring no particular response. An adolescent boy may say, "Am I supposed to just sit around and take it when my parents treat me like a baby?" He doesn't really expect an answer and will probably continue to express his feelings without interruption, thus showing that he was really not asking the therapist anything, but telling something.

The second type of question is a direct request for information, for example, "If I fail this English course, can I graduate?" Such a request should be answered with the appropriate data so the client can then use that information as he or she chooses. It would *not* be therapeutic to respond with, "You feel as though you may have to pass English in order to graduate."

The third type of question is the kind that would require the therapist to take responsibility for the child's behavior if he or she were to answer it, for example, "Should I run away from home?" or "Am I doing the right thing?" or "Should I tell on my friend?" Here, the therapist must explain directly to the child that he or she cannot answer such questions because that would be taking over; these are issues that the child must decide personally.

Certain questions are borderline questions, and the response given would have to depend on the stage of therapy. Perhaps the child will ask what the therapist really thinks about the child's dropping out of school. The therapist might respond by saying that such an action would put the student in a statistical category that would make it difficult to get a job and achieve the standard of living to which he or she has previously aspired. Such a response early in therapy, before the locus of responsibility had been clearly vested in the child, might place inappropriate responsibility within the therapist. But later on, such data might not be given too much weight by the child, and the therapist would therefore feel safe in responding and would not fear misinterpretation.

Dependency

Dependency in a child is often the greatest barrier to therapeutic progress, and the only way to combat it is through a kind of benevolent noncompliance.

Therapists cannot say, "Stop being dependent," because in so doing they take away responsibility and encourage dependency. They must simply refuse to become trapped into taking over. Thus, it is what therapists do *not* do that most often promotes the child's personal sense of responsibility.

> *Dana:* [*Age 17, speaking on the telephone*] Dr. Fisher? I just knew you wouldn't be in, but I wanted to talk to you before I do it.
> *Therapist:* I don't understand.
> *Dana:* I'm in Room 1207 of the Biltmore Hotel. I'm sitting in the window and as soon as I tell you goodbye, I'm going to jump and kill myself.
> *Therapist:* Sounds like you've reached a point of unbearable discouragement or depression.
> *Dana:* I have. I can't take it any longer. Besides, I'm not getting anywhere. Sometimes I feel so terrible I just want to tear my hair out or end it all, like right now. And besides . . . [*Pause*] nobody cares.
> *Therapist:* You don't think anyone has good feelings for you?
> *Dana:* Right—except maybe you. Everybody else thinks I'm such a dummy. Since I made all those Ds and Fs last semester, they just won't stay off my back. Now *they* know and *I* know and the whole world knows I'm a dummy.

The conversation continues for approximately 30 minutes, during which time the therapist empathizes with the client.

> *Therapist:* It's clear to me that we have a lot to talk over about how you feel—about your discouragement and about how other people including myself feel about you. Could we make an appointment tomorrow to go into this further?
> *Dana:* Yeah, I guess so.
> *Therapist:* Is 1:30 okay?
> *Dana:* Yeah.
> *Therapist:* Okay, then I'll see you in my office tomorrow at 1:30.
> *Dana:* Okay. Goodbye.
> *Therapist:* Goodbye.
> [*Next day at the 1:30 meeting*]
> *Dana:* I really can't believe this whole affair.
> *Therapist:* I don't think I know what you mean.
> *Dana:* I can't believe I'm really here and talking to you. You know I really did intend to kill myself. Everything I told you yesterday was true. I really was on the twelfth floor of the Biltmore, sitting in an open window when I called.

Therapist: I believed you.

Dana: I just knew that you would write your secretary a note so I couldn't hear you. You'd tell her to contact the hotel detective. She'd tell him that there was a suicide going on in 1207. Then I figured he'd come to the door, break it down and rush in and try to grab me. That would have been my cue; the minute he came through that door, I was going to jump. You're the only person who's ever had any confidence in me, and yesterday you had more confidence in me than I had in myself. I knew I was going to jump but you seemed to have confidence I wouldn't. I think that was the only thing that kept me from going out the window.

In this example the therapist conveyed to Dana that she was responsible for herself, and this was therapeutic. However, whenever a client threatens harm to self or others, the limits of responsibility are tested. In this case, the therapist assessed the situation and concluded that Dana was not in imminent danger. But had this conclusion not been reached, a different dialogue or different actions would have followed. Whenever a client may seriously harm self or another, the therapist must assume responsibility. It would *never*, for example, be therapeutic or ethically or legally appropriate not to intervene and protect a child from being seriously harmed or injured by an abusive parent.

Perhaps the most eloquent statement on the nature and extent of client responsibility was made by Rogers (1957). However, it must be remembered that this statement refers to adult clients and must be adapted for application to children.

> But is the therapist willing to give the client full freedom as to outcomes? Is he genuinely willing for the client to organize social or antisocial, moral or immoral? If not, it seems doubtful that therapy will be a profound experience for the client. Even more difficult, is he willing for the client to choose regression rather than accept it? . . . To me it appears that only as the therapist is completely willing that *any* outcome, *any* direction, may be chosen—only then does he realize the vital strength of the capacity and potentiality of the individual for constructive action. It is as he is willing . . . for neuroticism to be the choice, that a healthy normality is chosen. The more completely he acts upon his central hypothesis, the more convincing is the evidence that the hypothesis is correct.

The therapist's attitude toward the child's ability and right to determine the course of therapy is tested at almost every turn; there is always the temptation to push, probe, evaluate, and usurp; with a child, the temptation is greater because children are at a less responsible stage of development than adults. So let us focus on four errors that tend to usurp the locus of responsibility from the child—errors so common that they warrant special attention. In his book,

Techniques of Therapeutic Counseling, Porter (1950) expends considerable space showing inappropriate responses therapists often substitute for more appropriate ones. The four negative reactions he mentions are evaluating, interpreting, probing, and providing inappropriate support.

Evaluating

Passing judgment on a child's thoughts and actions is destined to retard the establishment of a positive relationship between therapist and child. Giving advice tells children you do not trust their ability to make decisions, and it can perform a disservice to empathy as well as to intimacy. A healthy, nondependent child cannot feel close to someone who is always giving advice, no matter how well-meaning; such advice always has a core of judgmental attitudes at the center, contaminating the whole.

Interpreting

Interpreting is similar to evaluating in that it is an easy trap for an unwary therapist to fall into. Most of the myths regarding therapy suggest that interpretation is important. A therapist who interprets or diagnoses a child's problems may stereotype the child and thereby respond to preconceived ideas, not to the child as an individual. Such responses may foster in the child negative feelings about self, thus diminishing both the therapist's valuing and the client's self-esteem. It can also create a false sense of security in both the therapist and the child. The child may think, "Ah, that's it. Now I know what the problem is, so maybe that will make everything all right." And the therapist might think: "Ah, that's it; now I have accurately diagnosed her, perhaps things will now fall into place." The truth is that they may be no better off after attaching the label than they were before. In fact, the labeling may interfere with therapeutic growth.

Experiential therapy is based on the assumption that *affect changes cognition* and not that *cognition changes affect.* Experiential therapists believe that when a child feels differently, he or she will begin thinking differently. Interpretation violates that assumption by trying to make the child think differently. The feelings a child gets from being interpreted or diagnosed are negative; they make the child feel devaluated and they interfere with feelings that bring about constructive personality reorganization.

Parents often find comfort in having their child's problem labeled as, say, a learning disability. There is a certain comfort in labeling, but it does not necessarily mean that help is forthcoming. Therapy is best conceived as an opportunity for the client to diagnosis him or herself. Anyone else's diagnosis, then, will be an interference. The therapist who begins diagnosing is tampering with the child's internal loci of evaluation, control, or responsibility, and thus is impairing the process of therapy.

Probing

The strongest tendency that many new therapists bring to therapy is the impulse to probe, and it is often the hardest habit to break. Because it is an attempt to direct the therapy, probing violates the principle of responsibility. The probing therapist is in actuality saying to the child, "I don't want to talk about what you want to talk about; why don't you talk about this instead? I know better than you what you should be talking about at this moment."

The point is subtle, but it pervades therapy. A natural conversational device, the probe must be replaced by empathy, which, as we have noted, comes less easily. The temptation to probe becomes greatest when therapy is problem-oriented rather than process-oriented. The therapist says, "Have you thought about this angle? When are you going to do this? What did you do then?" Ideally, when therapists become aware of the probing, a mental red light should appear to indicate that they have left the most effective process and become problem-oriented.

A question is a probe unless it is in the service of empathy. A typical empathic question would begin, "Am I understanding you correctly?" Any other question is a probe. Therapy is not a means of solving people's problems for them, or even helping them solve their most pressing one; it is a means of improving their problem-solving potential. When a child has a problem to solve, the temptation is to work on that specific difficulty rather than on the total child. It is when therapists work on the immediate problem, that they are inclined to probe.

Providing Inappropriate Support

The helper can be directly or indirectly supportive of a child. Indirect support, achieved by promoting relationship, congruence, valuing, empathy, and responsibility, provides a positive influence and increases the child's problem-solving potential. *Direct* support that is not based on reality is involved when the therapist says things like "Everything is going to be all right. It's not as bad as it seems." These are supportive statements but they do not provide supportive conditions. The most harmful direct support is that which is not based on reality, because it casts doubt on the therapist's credibility as well as on his or her judgement.

In general, any support provided directly rather than indirectly is discouraged because it vests the locus of evaluation outside the child. The ideal concept for the child to have is, "It's what I think and feel about myself that's important." Therefore, the therapist's supportive comments should be irrelevant unless they say, "I care; I understand." Saying that everything is going to be all right may only increase the client's defensiveness and thus his or her perception that things are not all right.

Understanding the bad feelings of a client, in all of their terribleness, may remove defenses, allowing for more objective, and thus realistic, perception. The child can then deal with problems directly. As such, the problems may be defused somewhat, since fantasy is always worse than reality.

Saying supportive things is not as valuable as showing interest in a child as an individual, listening to what he or she has to say, caring enough to empathize, to struggle to understand what the child is saying. To give support in these indirect ways is better than communicating it directly with direct statements, particularly ones that are not based on reality.

The following are examples of different responses that tend to usurp responsibility from a child. There are many appropriate responses; only one is given for each example.

Margo: My folks had a terrible fight the other night, and then I dreamed that Dad killed Mom.
Possible therapist responses:
Evaluating: We can really jump to silly conclusions sometimes, can't we?
Interpreting: Sometimes we act out in our dreams what we fear may happen in reality. You're very much afraid your father will harm your mother because they fight so much.
Probing: Very interesting. How did he do it?
Providing Inappropriate Support: Why, you know your father loves your mother; he'd never do anthing to harm her.
Providing Appropriate (Empathic) Support: It really scares you when your parents fight.

Andy: When those guys tease me about being short, I'm going to fight them.
Possible therapist responses:
Evaluating: Violence is never a solution.

Interpreting: You have a very short temper that seems to erupt at the slightest provacation.

Probing: Do they tease you in front of the girls?

Providing Inappropriate Support: You aren't that short.

Providing Appropriate Support: That really gets to you and you feel you just can't stand by and do nothing.

Sara: I don't want to stay here. I want to go to my Mommy.

Possible therapist responses:

Evaluating: That's not going to help. You need to be able to get by on your own.

Interpreting: Now you're just scared because this is all new. I won't hurt you.

Probing: Did your Mommy tell you something that makes you afraid of me?

Providing Inappropriate Support: Don't worry. Everything is going to be all right.

Providing Appropriate Support: It's not easy to do new things without your Mommy.

Susan: My folks gave Jill everything she asked for for Christmas, but they only gave me a jacket, when what I really wanted was a stereo.

Possible therapist responses:

Evaluating: You shouldn't assume that they like Jill better. Your jacket may have cost as much as her presents.

Interpreting: You may have an inferiority complex because you feel your sister is prettier than you are.

Probing: Did you have a big fight with them this week?

Providing Inappropriate Support: You're such a fine daughter, I know it couldn't be that they don't love you.

Providing Appropriate Support: You really are disappointed.

Todd: The team lost the game Saturday because I missed a fly ball in center field.

Possible therapist responses:

Evaluating: Now, don't sink into self-pity.

Interpreting: You must have a tendency to clutch under pressure.

Probing: What did the rest of the team have to say about that?

Providing Inappropriate Support: Oh, don't worry about it; everyone makes mistakes.

Providing Appropriate Support: That's an awfully heavy feeling, that you let the team down.

Richard: When I go out with these guys they always want to shoplift.

Possible therapist responses:

Evaluating: You've got to watch the kinds of friends you keep company with.

Interpreting: It's their way of showing they're grown up and beyond any authority.

Probing: Did you ever take anything?

Providing Inappropriate Support: I know you'd never do anything like that; you're just not that kind of guy.

Providing Appropriate Support: You sound stuck between wanting to be with your friends, but not wanting to break the law.

Diagnostic Testing and the Issue of Responsibility

Workers with children have traditionally spent a good deal of time administering psychological tests to children. Diagnostic tests can be useful in deciding whether children have a significant problem, whether they are in need of therapy, and what sort of therapy will suit the problem. Diagnostic testing is best done by someone other than the child's therapist. The therapeutic relationship requires one way of relating; the diagnostic relationship requires another. When doing a diagnostic evaluation, the worker must of necessity violate the principle of responsibility by demanding certain things of the child. Sometimes the child's responses must be accelerated with questions and probes. The adult becomes the leader, not the child, even with a simple IQ test. So if the child is diagnosed initially by the person who will eventually be the therapist, the child will have already established the understanding that the adult is in charge of the therapy hour. While the child's expectations and style of relating can be changed, much time and energy may be required to do so.

Therapy itself is one of the best diagnostic tools, and after a few sessions the therapist will probably know a great deal about the child. Without testing, the therapist will not know some potentially significant numbers (the specific IQ, Rorschach's F percent, the social maturity quotient, or the grade level placement) but will know what is most critical to therapy in the experiential sense (the client's capacity for intimacy, level of self-awareness, degree of congruence between perceived and ideal self, awareness of the locus of evaluation, and so on). And, once therapy begins, regardless of the diagnosis, the therapist will try to provide the good conditions that will promote growth.

4

Factors outside the Therapist-Client Relationship

Parents

Experiential therapy with a child usually begins with an assessment of the child in his or her family environment to determine where to begin and with whom to work. In some cases, a therapist may decide to see the parents instead of the child or to look for another way to alter the psychogenic forces at home. Under some conditions, more can be gained by working with parents than by working with the child. Sorting out where to begin requires an openness to working with children and their families.

Some therapists assume that the "fault" for the child's problems generally lies with the parents and focus on trying to change them. Such an attitude is more likely to be appropriate for a younger child whose environment is dominated by the parents. Few situations, however, are that simple, and often parents who voluntarily bring their children to therapy are full of guilt at having to do so. Those parents who do not feel guilty and who do not bring their children to therapy when it is needed may, indeed, be more likely to have personal problems that affect their child.

From our experience, it is far from correct to assume that a child's problem can always be traced to a deficiency in the parents. Some children's emotional development progresses well despite poor, even profoundly deficient parenting, while children who seem to have been raised in nurturing homes become maladjusted. Many times an unfortunate combination of parent and child traits make it difficult for the child to function and grow. There is seldom a single factor that can be pointed to as the cause of a child's problem.

Working successfully with a child is easier when there is a cooperative alliance with the parents. Before parents can cooperate with treatment they need to comprehend and accept recommendations. To make recommendations that are acceptable or understandable the therapist must identify the parents' situation, understand their point of view, and empathize with their feelings. Parents who seek psychological care for their child have most likely been attempting to help their child themselves for a long period of time. And, regardless of its effectiveness, parents have their own reasons for their style of parenting or way of relating to their children. The appropriate choice of intervention for parents must thus be tailored to the given situation and to the individual parents. Involvement with parents will then take many forms.

Counseling Parents

Parents may be seen separately to focus on the problems that interfere with their effective parenting or with the creation of a satisfactory and healthy home environment. For example, a mother concerned about her 5-year-old daughter's inability to be parted from her discovered through the course of her child's therapy that her daughter's problems mirrored her own. The mother chose to explore in individual therapy her own difficulties with separation and independence. This course of treatment was useful for both mother and child. It is not uncommon during the course of a child's therapy for a parent to realize a need for personal treatment.

Parents may also participate in marital therapy or family therapy. Family therapists have long written about children who act as scapegoats and who mask problems elsewhere. When pathology is inappropriately focused on a particular person rather than on the group's interrelationship, conjoint family therapy may be the most appropriate approach.

Therapists should also stay alert to a parent's using a child as a "ticket of admission" to therapy. Some parents are embarrassed to say, "I need help" and find it easier to say, "My child needs help." Such a style may be discernible early on. During an initial interview, for example, a mother may say that she is so distressed and frustrated with her child that she needs to talk with someone.

Parents may ask the therapist for training to enhance their parenting skills. Therapist and parents can work collectively to structure a growth-enhancing environment for the child. Parents spend many more hours with the child and are responsible for the atmosphere in which the child lives, so improving their parenting skills should have a major impact on the child. Effective parents create effective environments. Parent training can take many forms and may involve education, advice, or support.

While treating parents may be recommended, at times conditions are less than ideal. But even if the parents are unwilling or unavailable to enter therapy, and even if the therapist must try to help the child without any aid from the rest of the family, the therapist's efforts can still make an impact on the family. Despite obstacles, and with some limitations, this can be accomplished in several ways. As therapy progresses, the child's healthier behavior will begin to represent a different stimulus in the family environment. The family's altered responses may, in turn, augment the therapeutic impact and reinforce the child's adaptive behavior, making the child respond even more adaptively. The child can become the lever that moves the family toward health. It would be better if the fulcrum of psychotherapy could be used to change the entire family directly, but this is not always possible. Rather than give up when the family is uncooperative, the therapist must treat the child and be confident that some good can be accomplished.

Parent Consultation and Training

Parent consultation and training is one of the more effective means of intervention for many children's psychological problems (Wright, Schaefer, and Solomons 1979). Many parents can benefit from consulting a therapist about their child's minor behavioral or developmental problems. These difficulties need to be responded to so that the minor problems of development and adjustment in young children do not become major ones. Some parents also need to gain a better understanding of child development or to learn more effective ways of relating to or parenting children if their children's development is to progress along healthy lines. While the practices of the average parent are relatively effective, many of these parents may benefit from reassurance so that they can proceed in a more relaxed manner to rear a healthy child. More effective parents may also be interested in consultation or training to ensure that they establish a home environment that will best facilitate their child's healthy growth and development.

Parent consultation and training is generally a short-term, educational approach to dealing with a child's problems. Most therapists, regardless of their orientations, find it beneficial for many families. For the experiential therapist, parent consultation and training may be viewed as a treatment of choice for transient problems of adjustment or milder disruptions in a child's development. At other times it may be only one part of an intervention with a family or an important adjunct to a child's therapy.

Although parent consultation is different from experiential psychotherapy, the philosophical underpinnings, goals, and approaches of experiential psychotherapy can be relevant to these shorter term sessions. The good conditions for therapy will no doubt facilitate positive, healthy interactions with parents. Even sharing prescriptions for effective methods of toilet training will be enhanced if the therapist (or other service provider) empathizes with the parents' concerns and values the parents' and child's perspectives. When therapists share prescriptions they must always remember that parents are responsible for parenting. Therapists may share recommendations, but parents will decide whether or not to follow them. Experiential therapists may also find it useful to share with parents their way of conceptualizing child development and the related implications for how the parents might interact with their children to promote healthy development.

Most parents employ child-rearing strategies that grow naturally from their own experiences as children (Wright, Schaefer, and Solomons 1979). They tend either to recreate their own experiences and raise their children as they were raised or to react negatively to their own upbringing and rear their children in the opposite way. For example, if the parents' own parents were authoritarian, they become permissive, or vice versa. Similarly, if the parents were economically disadvantaged as children, they may provide excessive material goods to their children. Child-rearing strategies that are simply a reaction, either positive or negative, to the techniques of one's own parents can usually be improved. However, without parent consultation or training, improvement is not likely to occur.

Parent consultation may also represent a way of monitoring a child's condition. It can serve as a screening device and referral source for other methods of psychotherapeutic intervention. In some instances, parent consultation alone is a sufficient intervention, but many children will require other forms of therapy. Parent consultation provides an excellent opportunity for assessing the needs of both parents and children for other forms of therapy. Parent consultation can also assist the therapist in determining the prognosis for the parents or child to benefit from additional treatment.

Parents may seek counsel from a variety of professionals, but they are most likely to go to a primary (as opposed to specialty) health service provider such as a pediatrician or family physician. A report of the Task Force on Pediatric Education (American Academy of Pediatrics 1978) reviewed the results of a series of surveys asking where American families seek help for children's behavioral and psychological problems. These findings indicate that approximately 50 percent of American families have sought help for these problems from pediatricians. Pediatricians, thus, see two or three times as many patients for mental health problems as do psychologists and psychiatrists combined (Wright 1982).

One carefully conducted study further clarified the problems that children typically bring to primary health care settings. Duff, Rowe, and Anderson (1972) assessed all children who came to a pediatric clinic for treatment of physical disorders, psychological difficulties, or a combination of the two. The investigators found that 12 percent of the children had purely physical disorders, 36 percent had purely psychological difficulties, and 52 percent had a combination of the two. A representative survey of 1,200 mothers further delineated the areas for which parents are most likely to seek consultation (American Academy of Pediatrics 1978). Sixty-two percent of the mothers sought a pediatrician's counsel on problems with the child's growth and development, 49 percent needed help in coping with discipline and behavior problems, and 42 percent asked for assistance in dealing with the child's learning difficulties.

Primary mental health care differs from traditional psychological service in several basic ways. In primary health care settings, more clients are seen, less time is spent with each client, and the clients generally possess less debilitating forms of mental disorder. Most parents seeking primary mental health care services for a child are getting, at best, 5–15 minutes of listening and direct advice. At worst, parents are being told routinely that the child will outgrow the problem and that the parents should not concern themselves lest they make the problem worse. In fact, the modal form of mental health care which our society offers a consumer or client is 5–15 minutes of direct advice provided by a nonpsychiatric physician once or twice a year.

Such findings suggest various recommendations to ensure appropriate support for parents. Psychologists, counselors, pediatricians, and other health service providers need to work together to assist parents in rearing psychologically healthy children. Appropriate referral networks from primary to specialty care (and vice versa) must be established to optimize care. Attention to the conditions of effective parenting should also be an essential part of the practice of all physical or mental health service providers who work with children and families. Indirect treatment by means of parent consultation is a practical approach to meeting the physical and mental health needs of large numbers of children. Focusing on parenting skills and a child's home environment may be what a child needs most to develop and progress.

Child–rearing is every nation's most important task. Approximately 5 million children are born in the United States each year; over 50 million parents are engaged in rearing over 75 million children under the age of 15. The future of our nation, whether it thrives or even survives, depends upon how we socialize the young. Socializing the young is in turn determined primarily by parents and their child–rearing strategies. Yet, despite the need and importance of excellence in parenting, resources for parents remain limited. The widespread use of parent consultation and training as a preventive technique and as a way to assist those children suffering from emotional and behavioral problems, should be encouraged. Frequent, even annual participation in a parent consultation program or a parenting clinic might be considered to be as worthwhile and important as the annual pediatric physical checkup (Wright, Schaefer, and Solomons 1979).

Working with Groups of Parents

The natural tendency of parents to discuss child-rearing problems with other parents can be channeled into productive group discussions or group sessions for parent training. Various models of parent training are available, and parent training may range along a continuum from group therapy to group guidance. Whatever the flavor of the group, ideally it will provide parents with knowledge of and a feeling for the good conditions for parenting.

Experiential parent training groups may be structured in various ways. Typically, parent groups meet for an hour weekly over a 6- to 10-week period. Consistent with general principles of group therapy, groups ideally will consist of six to twelve parents. Our experience suggests that some general groupings of parents in terms of their needs and level of functioning may facilitate group interactions. Relatively healthy parents concerned with enhancing a child's development may not, for example, readily mix with parents who are suspected of abusing or neglecting a child and who have been ordered by the court to attend treatment. The needs of such diverse parents might best be met by grouping them with somewhat similar parents. This approach, of course, must always be weighed against the potential value of exposure to parents with highly diverse backgrounds, experiences, and needs. Because of their availability, there are generally more mothers than fathers in groups. In two-parent families both parents should attend and each should be expected to participate.

During the first group session, the therapist and the parents introduce themselves to one another. Introductions may include information about the parent (i.e., name, age, and reason for attending the group) and the child (i.e., name, age, and problem). Group goals and methods will also be discussed. Subsequent meetings can focus on effective parenting and ways to facilitate the healthy development of children. The principles of experiential therapy—intimacy, congruence, valuing, locus of responsibility, and empathy—represent the good conditions for development and growth and should be shared with parents. Ideally, these principles will not just be discussed by the group but will be experienced by the group as well. Experiencing these principles within a supportive group setting may help parents to translate them into the home setting.

Group sessions may begin with parents describing episodes with their children that have occurred at home during the past week. In early sessions the therapist may be more didactic and may attempt to share examples of more adaptive or healthier parenting styles. The focus is typically on teaching parents to relate to their children in new ways that will facilitate the child's growth.

The middle sessions of most parent training groups typically involve less teaching and more modeling of skills such as empathy, positive regard, and the avoidance of rejection. In later sessions, group members often assume responsibility for most of the sharing and teaching. The group members' feelings of allegiance, rapport, and support for one another often intensify during this stage.

Throughout the series of sessions the therapist serves as a facilitator, promoting group cohesion and inviting and encouraging the expression of various viewpoints. Through participation in the group the parents may receive support and ideas from peers as well as from the therapist. Parents may also be able to discover important principles by interacting with, observing, and listening to other parents. Over the years, the practice of parent consultation and training has revealed some subtleties that can enhance its effectiveness. For instance, the group should be concerned with principles and not "cookbook" solutions (Wright 1978). Parents frequently ask specific questions, such as "What should I do when my child . . . " Consultants or therapists who attempt to answer these questions directly find that parents have far too many individual questions to permit specific responses for each. On the other hand, if parents master basic principles and receive support in generalizing these principles to a variety of situations, then all members of the group benefit. A Chinese proverb observes, "Give a man a fish and you feed him for a day; teach him to fish and you feed him for life." A therapist or consultant who attempts to answer every question can only provide short-term help, but one who provides parents with an understanding of human behavior and with principles for effective parenting has given them something of long-term value.

Another useful technique for parent training or consultation is the use of mnemonic devices, including humor, to improve parents' recall. A friendly, supportive, even humorous atmosphere has other benefits as well. Not only is the group experience more pleasant, but the atmosphere may also relax many guilt-ridden parents and enhance their learning.

Modeling has proved to be another effective method for group parent training. Here an appropriate child-rearing response is not discussed abstractly but is demonstrated for the parents. This method is particularly effective with parents from lower socioeconomic classes, because many of these parents do not have the verbal facility necessary to understand esoteric principles of human behavior. Seeing such principles demonstrated allows these parents to assimilate them more easily. Mira (1970) has reported that fewer sessions are required when modeling is used.

At the end of group consultation parents typically follow one of three courses. Some parents want further consultation or training designed for more advanced participants. Others express a desire to enter a more psychotherapy-oriented group, one that will focus on the parents themselves and on their problems. A remaining group seeks no further help. Although attrition is usually minimal once the groups are under way, not all parents to whom parent training is offered or recommended agree to participate.

Group parent training may meet many parents' needs. Working with groups of parents is also an economical use of time. A therapist who provides individual psychotherapy reaches one child in an hour-long session. In contrast, group consultation enables the therapist to work with many mothers and fathers in one hour. If the therapist works with seven mothers or fathers who have an average of three children each, then twenty-one children may be helped. Although all of these children may not have serious emotional or behavioral problems, enhancing their development is certainly a worthy objective. At the conclusion of most parent group programs, parents typically report that they have altered the environment of their children three or four hours a day as a result of their participation. This may mean that the one hour of professional time invested by the therapist or consultant now affects those twenty-one children for twenty-one to twenty-eight hours per week, making an average of over five hundred hours of difference in children's experience per week. An added benefit of group consultation is that it makes the fee per visit more affordable for parents.

Several investigators of group parent training and consultation have demonstrated the effectiveness of this method for changing parental attitudes and promoting children's adjustment (Hereford 1963; Carkhuff and Bierman 1970; Wright 1976). Reviews of the process of parent consultation have concluded that parent training programs are effective, and the validity of this technique should be well established (Berkowitz and Graziano 1972; Johnson and Katz 1973). These approaches are ideally suited for coping with the many requests by parents of essentially normal children for handling the everyday problems of child development and adjustment.

The use of parent consultation has expanded greatly in recent years, and reviews and summaries of these activities are available (Wright, Schaefer, and Solomons 1979). One particularly popular structured training program has been the Parent Effectiveness Training (PET) program. Gordon (1971) developed PET, a franchised system for teaching parent effectiveness. This method relies on the principles of personality and social development espoused by Gordon and his former colleague, Carl Rogers. Therapists or other individuals wishing to use this method are trained, certified, and then franchised to offer parent effectiveness courses throughout the United States. The widespread sale of Dr. Gordon's book and the large number of participants in Parent Effectiveness Training programs attest to the popularity of this program.

Other Methods of Training Parents

Parent consultation is by no means the only available method for treating children indirectly through training parents. Books for parents may be quite useful when parents need general information regarding child development or effective ways of parenting (Wright 1978). If parents are guided toward appropriate books, they can learn part or all of the information that they need on their own. Bibliotherapy provides detailed, comprehensive material to parents and can minimize the need for professional involvement. The primary virtue of bibliotherapy, however, is that little is lost in trying it. If reading a relevant, appropriate book can eliminate the need for a portion of a therapy session, enough money has been saved to buy the book. Even when bibliotherapy is not sufficient to meet all the parent's needs, the book may still provide a framework on which to base a consultation session and make it more productive. Bibliotherapy may also be used as part of a more involved therapeutic relationship with parents.

An increasing number of books is available to parents who wish to improve their child-rearing skills. Books that may be useful to parents include some standard reference works as well as some newer ones: A. Gesell, *Studies in Child Development* (New York: Harper Brothers, 1948); H. G. Ginott, *Between Parent and Child* (New York: Macmillan Co., 1968); B. Spock, *Baby and Child Care* (New York: Hawthorn, 1968); B. Brazelton, *Infants and Mothers: Differences in Development* (New York: David McKay Co., 1972); and L. Salk, *What Every Child Would Like His Parent to Know* (New York: Dell, 1969).

Recently a number of other parent training techniques have emerged (Wright, Schaefer, and Solomons 1979). Some practitioners have relied on television and the mass media to convey their message to parents. Gordon (1976) and Wright (1970) have each developed a series of educational television programs designed to assist parents with their child-rearing problems. Other techniques for indirect treatment include cassette recordings and leaderless discussion groups. Another promising method for improving parenting skills is "monitored play therapy" (Golden 1969; Rogers 1969). With this approach parents are allowed to watch, through a one-way vision mirror, a psychotherapist interacting with their child. In this way, parents do not merely hear about the kind of interaction most likely to facilitate healthy personality development in children—the techniques are demonstrated for them.

Parental Involvement in a Child's Treatment

In many instances, it is beneficial to involve the parents directly in the treatment of a child. Such strategies are particularly useful when working with younger children. The history of child psychotherapy is full of examples of parents' being actively involved with their child's treatment. Freud (1959), in "Analysis of a Phobia in a Five-Year-Old Boy," wrote that: "the treatment itself was carried out by the child's father. . . . No one else, in my opinion, could possibly have prevailed on the child to make such avowals; the special knowledge by means of which he was able to interpret the remarks made by his five-year-old son was indispensable, and without it the technical difficulties in the way of conducting a psychoanalysis upon so young a child would have been insuperable" (p. 149). Freud thus recognized the potency of the parent-child relationship and chose to capitalize on it in this classic case study. While contemporary child psychoanalysis does not typically use the parents in the treatment process, there is still the understanding that involvement with parents may have therapeutic benefit.

Other treatment modalities have also acknowledged the potential usefulness of parental involvement in therapy for children. Behavior therapists are especially likely to involve parents in the treatment of specific child behavior problems. The behavior therapist may conceptualize such treatment not within the traditional dyadic model (therapist and client) but within a triadic model, which directly involves the parents (Tharp and Wetzel 1969). The therapist and the parents may develop a treatment plan for the child together; this plan is then typically implemented by the parent and monitored by the therapist, who may have little or no direct contact with the child. In such programs, parents are actively involved at all times with their child's treatment.

Nondirective and experiential therapists have also incorporated parents into child treatment programs. Baruch (1949) and Moustakas (1959) suggested that play sessions at home may be a way of fostering good parent-child relationships. And since growing up is never easy, parents may be able to structure play therapy sessions to help their child overcome or cope with some of the normal growing pains.

Natalie Fuchs (1957) described such a process in her recounting of a series of successful home play therapy sessions with her one-and-a-half year old daughter. Fuchs, with the support of her father, Carl Rogers, helped her daughter to overcome a toilet-training problem. Experiential approaches have also been extended to involve parents in the treatment of the emotionally disturbed child. Guerney (1964; Stover and Guerney 1967) has pioneered the area of filial therapy, or the training of parents as psychotherapists for their own children. Guerney's (1964) "filial therapy" approach trains groups of six to eight parents to conduct play sessions with their emotionally disturbed young children and to act as client-centered therapists for them. Carkhuff and Bierman (1970) have also attempted to provide parents with psychotherapeutic skills designed to aid them in working with their own children.

While the styles of parental involvement in treatment may vary, such involvement should mobilize the parents in constructive ways. Involving the parents may minimize their resistance to bringing a child to a therapist. When parents start their children in therapy, they often feel inadequate to provide the necessary help or assistance to their child, and they may even believe that they are the cause of their child's problems. Through involvement in a child's treatment, parents may come to recognize that their help is vital, so they may be better motivated to help therapy to progress. Maintaining an alliance with the parents is often essential for the continued support of the child's treatment. Active involvement may also expose the parents to new, more successful, and more rewarding ways of interacting with their child.

Confidentiality

Confidentiality has long played an important role in psychotherapy. A client who fears that what he or she confides will be divulged to others will not communicate with and relate to the therapist freely. When working with adult clients, issues of confidentiality can be immediately and often easily dealt with. The client is initially advised of the therapist's valuing of confidentiality (although some limits may be briefly acknowledged). When working with children and parents, however, confidentiality is not so simple.

Parents do not always appreciate the importance of confidentiality to a child's therapy. When working with a young child, the parents may expect and request that information the child shares in private with the therapist be freely available to them. Such attitudes are further complicated by legal rights of parents and guardians. Boundaries and limits of confidentiality need to be set and discussed with everyone involved.

Young children may have varying expectations about confidentiality. Some young children do not perceive a need for privacy and indeed themselves share intimate aspects of treatment with their parents, siblings, and others. These children have not read books on ethics and professionalism. Others assume a conspiracy between parent and therapist. For them, shared confidences are perceived as betrayal, and sharing information with parents clearly impairs the child-therapist relationship. Adolescents in particular are likely to be extremely sensitive to issues of confidentiality. Within treatment, adolescents require privacy and place a high value on it, perhaps because of their need to become separate from their parents and because of their wish to "become their own person."

Confidentiality, then, can clearly make an impact on the therapeutic relationship. The boundaries and limits of confidentiality can be discussed from the start with the child and the parents. For most children, however, the therapist's actions over time will be more important than discussions. Children, more than adults, may have difficulty believing that what they say in therapy is confidential. A child grows up believing that adults confide in one another and share information. Mother tells Dad about the bad thing Johnny did today; the teacher tells the parents when he gets in a fight; the dentist tells the parents that Johnny hasn't been brushing, and so on. It will take the child a while to understand that the therapist's loyalty is to him or her; the child will test this premise over and over before believing.

Because of possible conflicts of interest when working with children and parents, therapists may need to structure sessions so as to minimize problems of confidentiality. It might be advisable never to meet with the child's parents unless the child is present. In some instances, if a child's parent is in individual treatment, it might be preferable for the parent to see someone other than the child's therapist. Even if the child gives permission for his or her own therapist to see the parents in separate sessions, this may still be inappropriate if a separation makes an intimate relationship with the child impossible. Even if the therapist were scrupulous in not revealing confidences, the appearance would be there; when the child sees the parents with the therapist, or simply knows they are in contact, suspicions may arise. Attention to the appropriate structuring of therapy sessions is necessary to foster the development of the essential therapeutic relationship.

Experiential Parenting

The goal of experiential psychotherapy—to foster the natural unfolding of the self-actualizing behaviors inherent within each individual—is similar to the goals of effective parenting. Most parents are concerned about the growth, healthy development, and fulfillment of their children. The principles of experiential therapy may then be as useful to parents as to therapists, and familiarization with intimacy, congruence, valuing, locus of responsibility, and empathy may provide useful guidelines to parents in their day-to-day interactions with their children.

Some parents who wish to focus more directly on their relationship with their child may structure experiential play sessions at home. Guerney (1976) developed a training manual for parents for this purpose. The following are some guidelines for parents who want to use play sessions at home to enhance their relationship with their child and to facilitate their child's emotional growth. Play sessions are most appropriate for parents with children between the ages of three and ten years. While experiential play sessions at home may be helpful, they will not replace a child's therapy or a family's treatment. Parents who have real concerns regarding a child's development should seek professional consultation and should use structured experiential play sessions at home only as part of a total treatment plan.

Selecting a Time: Since play sessions are to be different from normal parent-child interactions, some structure will be important. Selecting a special time will help orient the child to the uniqueness of this period. The time must suit both parent and child, must be free from distractions and interruptions, and should be a regular event that the child can expect and count on. Frequency of sessions may be determined to meet the needs of the parent and child. For a normal child who is not experiencing or facing an immediately stressful event, one half-hour session per week might be sufficient. For a child trying to cope with more stressful events (i.e., birth of a sibling, starting school, moving, divorce) sessions might be longer or more frequent.

Selecting a Place: Selecting a place for home play sessions will also help define and set boundaries for a new relationship. Rules for structuring a therapeutic environment are appropriate for both clinic and home playroom (see "The Therapeutic Environment" in this chapter). Since the relationship between the child and parent will be the focus of home play sessions, the environment should be designed to enhance that relationship. Although healthy relationships can flourish anywhere, some settings can facilitate and enhance the parent-child relationship. The place selected should be free from distractions—television, other siblings, and day-to-day household happenings can distract and interfere with relating at the moment, so removing parent and child from such distractions should be a part of home play session structure. The environment chosen should also suit the needs of the child. For example, children who like and need to act things out motorially may require room to move. Children who like to express things graphically through drawings and paintings may require a room or spot that can tolerate a spill. In almost every home there is at least one area that is appropriate for home play sessions. It is not expected that the setting will duplicate the clinic playroom, but it should be a useful home setting that facilitates the parent-child relationship.

Choosing Toys and Games: Toys and games should be selected to promote relational growth. As such, how a toy is used is more important than what toy is used. Parents can select inexpensive and durable toys that are appropriate for use in the home. Guidelines for the selection of toys in a clinic (see "The Therapeutic Environment") may provide useful pointers to parents, but again it is not expected that all of the supplies of the clinic playroom will be duplicated at home.

Toy selection will also need to be based in part on the child's developmental level. For example, a young child may not have sufficient fine motor control for pencil or crayon drawings but may enthusiastically communicate with finger paints. Similarly, older children may be offended if they are expected to play with toys they consider childish. While toy selection should be individually suited to the child and the home, some toys may be especially appropriate. Paper, crayons, paint, and clay facilitate graphic communication and are especially suited to the 4- to 10-year-old child. Through their drawings and artistic creations, children may share thoughts that are difficult for them to put into words. Parents might hear through drawings what might otherwise not be said.

Dolls and doll houses and puppets that represent members of the family can promote the exploration of family relations in spontaneous dramatic play. A young child playing house may recreate self, family, and day-to-day events in a fashion that permits understanding, acceptance, and growth; an older child might express the same feelings about family life by creating and acting out plays. Dart guns or a Bozo doll might be included in the playroom since they encourage the expression of aggressive feelings that may be especially difficult for parents and children to deal with directly. Other toys may be equally useful and will be discussed more completely later in this chapter.

Toys selected for home play sessions may be restricted for use only in the play session. Guerney (1976) suggests that toys should not be removed or added once sessions have begun. Such rules can be of value if they emphasize the specialness of a home play session. Parental judgment must be used to determine the structure and rules that can best facilitate the parent-child relationship.

Getting Started: Play sessions begin with explanations and initiations. Parental explanations will vary somewhat depending on the age of the child. Younger children cannot comprehend lengthy, abstract reasons, so instructions for them must be simply stated, and the parent may want to say, "I would like to have some special play times with you." For older children, more information may be necessary and useful. A parent might say to an older child, "I want to spend more time with you" or "I would like to get to know you in a more special way." The explanations may also vary depending on the reasons for the play sessions. For a normal child whose parents are concerned with notions of actualization, introductions may be brief and fairly direct. For more disturbed children, the home play session may be one of a series of intervention efforts for the child. The child may have been referred to a child therapist, and the problems identified may be as apparent to the child as to the parents. For such a child, home play sessions may be one part of a more comprehensive intervention plan, but the parents' explanations can still be simple. For this disturbed child the emphasis remains on the desire to be together and to improve the relationship. Following an introduction most children readily participate. Complete parental attention is highly reinforcing to most children and something that most find exciting and special.

The Parental Role: The parental role in home play sessions is to create the necessary and sufficient conditions for growth in the child. These conditions have been previously discussed, and here we need only acknowledge their importance to parenting. The presence of the following conditions within the play sessions creates the ideal setting.

1. The child and parent are in intimate psychological contact.
2. The parent is congruent in the relationship.
3. The parent experiences and communicates unconditional positive regard for the child.
4. The parent experiences the child's internal frame of reference empathically and communicates this awareness to the child.
5. The parent not only allows, but requires, that the locus of responsibility for the child's behavior be vested in the child.

Most important is the attitude with which the parent approaches the play sessions. The parent must be empathic, must value the child unconditionally, and must respect the child's right of self-determination. Most importantly, the parent must be genuine or congruent.

It is to be hoped that the parent will establish an atmosphere of free play and acceptance for the child. In such a setting the child may become aware of feelings and may have an opportunity to express them either verbally or through play. The child should be permitted to express hate, anger, love, joy, and resentment, and should feel free to do so. Parental acceptance of the child's feelings is essential and can help the child come to a better understanding of how to deal with them. For many parents, hearing these feelings is difficult, and accepting a child's feelings may be frightening at first. The play sessions should also help the parents gain a greater awareness of their own feelings toward the child and should give them a chance to explore and accept these feelings.

Since dealing with feelings may be frightening, parents can be advised that home play sessions might in some ways be different from other parent-child interactions. Some behaviors that would be inappropriate at other times and places may be permissible, even highly desirable within a home play session. Direct and immediate disclosure of feelings, for example, may not always be desirable in everyday life. Children can quickly learn that play sessions are different and special and that certain things may be permissible only there. The improvement of the parent-child relationship should, however, certainly extend beyond the boundaries of the play session. Through such sessions children and their parents may use their own resources more effectively so that they can live with one another in greater harmony.

The Therapeutic Environment

The relationship between therapist and child is always the focus of therapy, and that relationship is what brings about the desired personality reorganization. The therapeutic environment, then, should be designed to enhance that relationship. An inexperienced therapist may place more emphasis than is warranted on the room and the available toys and games; it is easy to use these things as crutches. Good therapy, however, can happen anywhere—in a well-designed setting, or under a tree, or in a boiler room for that matter. Toys and games, running water, and a playhouse may, of course, be quite useful to therapy; if they are, they should be available and should be used to the child's benefit.

Suiting the Environment to the Young Child

The environment chosen for therapy should depend on the age of the child, the nature of the child's problems, and the stage of the therapeutic relationship. Young children who seem to have a lot of acting-out to do may do best in a well-designed room. Children who come from very structured environments and are confined by many rules may benefit from a less rigid enclosure, and the relationship might be enhanced in a park or on long walks. Each setting provides its own opportunities and limitations, so the therapist must be sensitive and creative in deciding which is appropriate to the child's needs at that moment.

The ideal room for young children is scaled to them. The sinks, pictures, and shelves must be at their level, as should the tables and chairs. This can be accomplished most effectively with a six-figure federal grant, but barring that, many satisfactory environments can be improvised. Some have found it simpler to raise the floor than to lower everything else. Platforms in front of sinks can suffice if necessary. The room should be soundproof and childproof, washable and malletproof—reasonably indestructible. Windows should be protected. Wiring for video- and audiotaping and a one-way mirror will increase the possible uses for the room. The child, of course, must always know when such teaching devices are being used.

Suiting the Environment to the Older Child and Adolescent

Older children and adolescents may not feel comfortable in a scaled-down room or in a playroom. Offending clients by selecting a setting they consider childish will not facilitate rapport. Informal rules suggest that play therapy is most appropriate for the young- and middle-childhood ages, and the upper age limit for play therapy is about twelve years. Such an age limit is, however, certainly not a rigid rule but a general suggestion. Adolescents may occasionally, have special needs that are best met in a playroom. Information about the clients' interests and favorite activities can help the therapist make decisions about the therapeutic environment, and, of course, the clients can always be asked where they would be comfortable.

While older children and adolescents may not feel comfortable in a playroom, they may feel equally uncomfortable in the more sterile adult therapy room designed primarily for talk-oriented therapies. Adolescence is a transitional period of development, and the therapeutic environment can be structured with this in mind. Such environments should be informal, with age-appropriate activities and comfortable furniture available. Since some adolescents find a 50-minute session an interminable period of time to talk with their therapist, some activity may be useful. A bumper pool table may permit action as well as interaction. More advanced games can be included in a cabinet to draw upon as needed. Because adolescents are especially concerned with relating to peers, group therapy might be useful, especially for adolescents who relate more easily to peers than to therapists.

Choosing Toys and Games

Certain guidelines should be followed when choosing toys and games. It is essential that the materials be age-appropriate and that they elicit feeling and promote relationship. For small children, the expression of feelings of power or anger may be induced by their playing with dolls, puppets, soldiers, or toy motorcycles; for older children, the stimuli may be pictures, books, or competitive games such as Monopoly or bumper pool. Consider the primary sources of affect, and choose toys and games likely to elicit them. Dart guns are effective elicitors of aggression, as is a boxing bag or an inflatable Bozo. Projects like model plane building require cooperation and can effectively encourage intimacy. The toys should not be fragile or battery-powered, since toys that break or run down can cause distractions and frustration. Clay, finger paints, water, and sand, are valuable. The following list gives other potentially useful toys and games.

dolls	table games (cards, checkers, etc.)
doll house and furniture	toy guns, knives, darts
nursing bottles	punching bag or doll
puppets	toy soldiers
costumes	bumper pool table
toy animals	books
paper	toy telephone
paints	play money
crayons	blocks or building toys
balls	pipe cleaners
blackboard and chalk	

Virginia Axline, in her book *Play Therapy* (1947), suggests appropriate toys and games and points out that the therapist must be responsible for the order of the room and equipment before the client enters and must be certain that a previous client's use of the material will not influence the next client.

Another factor to be considered when choosing games is their usefulness in facilitating relationship. Certain kinds of games and activities tend to isolate people, and others tend to bring people together. People who play checkers, for instance, often retreat into themselves and ponder their next move. Monopoly, on the other hand, can bring out a lot of feeling, not all of it friendly, and the players always seem to have plenty to talk, laugh, or yell at one another about. Such interaction can be fruitful material for alert therapists, who are always concerned with what is happening between them and the child at the moment.

Playing games like Monopoly can be productive or not, depending on the child and the therapist. The two can get entangled in winning and losing, in which case the game becomes isolating; but a skilled therapist can use it to learn what is going on within the child or between the two of them at the time. The therapist may say, "Wow, you're really beating me and that seems to feel good." or, "You feel you made a bad decision and that makes you angry." Whether anything is a device for fostering intimacy depends on the human beings involved. The therapist must know him or herself as well as the child and must choose age-appropriate activities that elicit feelings and foster interaction.

Most importantly, the therapist must use the activity therapeutically, never allowing it to control therapeutic activity. The good therapist can find expressions of feeling anywhere, but it is helpful to structure activity in a manner that facilitates the search. In relationship therapy, the way an activity promotes relationship is the most important criterion. The ideal activity is a catalyst that fosters interaction that ultimately increases the intensity of the relationship between the child and the therapist, beginning with the first session and prevailing until the last.

The First and Last Sessions

Some therapists are most comfortable beginning a therapeutic relationship with a structured interview. They tell the child what therapy is going to be like, explain the limits, or outline the sources of help they expect to draw from. The therapist might say that the two of them will have a relationship that the therapist hopes will be deep and will help the child grow and adapt; he or she may promise to be honest with the child, to be caring, and to try to understand empathically what the child is feeling. The therapist might even promise not to diagnose or interpret, but to simply understand, and might explain that responsibility for the child's actions will rest within the child.

Such explanations may be useful as a way of establishing the tone of the sessions, but most children neither understand nor benefit from a mere description of the five good conditions of experiential psychotherapy—they must experience them. Children must experience intimacy before they can relax their defenses. They must have to make decisions before they will *feel* responsible, and they must feel responsible before they will begin to *act* responsibly. Some minimal structuring, however, may facilitate relating and can be helpful when therapy begins.

Exchanging Expectations

Clients and therapists bring various expectations with them to the therapy process. Since these expectations have long been known to affect the process and outcome of therapy, some understanding of them can be helpful (Frank 1959, 1971, 1973; Goldstein 1962a, 1966). Two major classes of expectations of the therapy process have been defined and investigated.

Goldstein (1962b) delineated the difference between prognostic and participant role expectancies. Prognostic expectancy is the degree of improvement anticipated by the client or by the therapist. A child, for example, may expect magical outcomes following a meeting with a therapist. The therapist, however, most likely will expect other outcomes for the session. Participant role expectancies are the anticipations held by the therapist and client regarding the behaviors expected of each participant in the therapeutic relationship. For example, a child may approach a therapist with visions of being disciplined, reprimanded, repaired, nurtured, and comforted. Therapists, in turn, have their own notions of how they should behave while relating to a child.

Almost every client, young or old, comes to therapy with unrealistic expectations. Inaccurate or inappropriate role expectations or misunderstandings about treatment are related to premature terminations or dropouts at child psychiatric and guidance clinics (Farley, Peterson, and Spanos 1975; Levitt 1958; Richardson and Cohen 1968). Early attention to fostering realistic expectations may be useful and may reduce the likelihood of premature terminations (Bonner and Everett, 1982, in press; Day and Reznikoff 1980; Holmes and Urie 1975). Some initial clarification of expectations may thus be necessary to get therapy started and to keep it going.

Many children and their parents come to therapy thinking that the therapist will cure the child. One of the most pervasive ideas in the United States is that some people are experts and that when something goes wrong one must find an expert to fix it. A child coming to therapy may bring this idea either from his or her own expectations or from those of the caretakers. Certainly the parents will think, "My child is broken. Fix him." Even some therapists come to therapy with this idea of themselves. The problem with such a belief is that it is the antithesis of the principle of responsibility. Such an idea cannot be argued away in the first session. In order for therapy to be as effective as possible, the therapist must always remember that young Bobby is and always will be the world's number one expert on himself. Bobby must reexperience week after week that he is responsible for the content of the therapy hour and for his own ideas and feelings; he cannot be told. So in the initial hour, instead of giving a dissertation on locus of responsibility, the therapist should begin the relationship by making some simple statement such as, "This is your hour to do with as you please" and then sticking to actions that reinforce that idea.

Without doing any formal structuring, the therapist can express certain expectations in the first interview to set the tone. For instance, one of the best ways to begin therapy is to pick up a nonverbal cue from the child and then respond empathically by saying, "I'll bet you're wondering what's going on here, what this is all about, and how we're going to operate." The child will often say "yes," and then the therapist can say when they will meet, describe the games and activities available, and emphasize that the decision as to how the time is used will be made by the child.

The issue that often arises first is the question of why the child is there. At the beginning, the therapist might say, congruently, that he or she is curious about what the child believes is the reason for their coming together. This is for the therapist's benefit, but may ultimately be of use to the child. Children who receive no guidance from their parents are rarely prepared for the experience of psychotherapy. Parents are often confused about what to tell a child, and that confusion, combined with a tendency to retreat from difficulty, may result in their telling the child nothing. The child may simply be dumped at the therapist's office, or may be told he or she is going to the doctor's, which conjures up a totally inappropriate set of images concerning shots, stethoscopes, and physical examinations.

Children as a group tend not to be psychologically minded; they will not see themselves as neurotics or psychotics. Even if they do perceive a problem, their perceptions will not resemble anything in a textbook on psychopathology. They can, however, understand certain ideas if they are presented in appropriate language, for example, "You're here because your parents are concerned that you aren't doing well in school and no one can figure out why. Your parents and teachers know that you're smart enough to learn, so something must be getting in your way. You're here so we can work on that." Happiness and unhappiness are concepts that children can understand, certainly if they are of school age, so the therapist might say, "Your parents feel that you aren't very happy and that coming here might help."

It is crucial that at some level the therapist understand a client's conception of why he or she is there, and to do so the therapist may have to express this curiosity congruently and empathize with nonverbal expressions that seem to be related to this topic. Most importantly, the child must know clearly the point of the sessions is psychotherapy; the purpose is not simply to play games or to become friends, although those things may happen. The first session fails if the child does not realize that some important people in the child's life feel that there is a need and that the therapist is there to work with the child on that need, provided it actually exists and to the extent that the child is willing to work. Establishing these points can be very important to therapy's getting off in the right direction.

Children often deny having any problem at the first session. Therapists can respond empathically, reserving the right to decide whether they believe there is a problem or not. Such denials from clients are opportunities for empathy, opportunities for therapists to show that they understand that the clients would rather be somewhere else. Actually, it does not matter if there is a specific problem or not. All of us have room to grow. The upgrading of essentially normal behavior is one appropriate goal for psychotherapy. There are occasions, often early in a therapeutic relationship, when this idea should be conveyed.

Children rarely make the decision to go into therapy; it is made for them. Before the first hour they should be told that they must go to therapy, but if they are still unconvinced by the first session that therapy is necessary, they may be reluctant even to enter the room. Perhaps they will stand in the hallway and refuse to come in. This situation can be used as another opportunity for the therapist to empathize with the clients' fury or fear. As soon as the therapist encounters the child in the waiting room or in the hallway the first session has begun. The therapist's task is to provide the good conditions for growth and adaptation at all times, in all places.

Exchanging expectations with parents is also needed when a child's therapy begins. Parental expectations are another important ingredient in the child's treatment process (Day and Reznikoff 1980; Bonner and Everett in press; Weiss and Dlugokinski 1974). Parents may approach their child's therapist with various feelings and expectations that may need to be explored. By bringing a child to therapy, the parents may be acknowledging that they alone cannot meet this child's needs. This child's development is not progressing as the parents think or wish it would. They may view the therapist as a rival, a more effective parent who can better meet the child's needs. Parents may, furthermore, experience guilt over their child's difficulties and expect to be blamed for them. Helping parents work with these issues is important to their adjustment as well as to that of their child. While some parental attitudes and expectations may be talked about during a first session, this is usually just a beginning. Parents will need to experience acceptance over time before guilt and blame can dissipate.

Exchanging expectations of the structure of treatment can be useful early on. Parents and therapists may have differing expectations of how a child's therapy should be arranged or structured. A survey conducted by Woods (1978) obtained normative data on the expectations of mothers and child psychotherapists about the process of child psychotherapy. Woods found some differences in parental and therapist expectations that could be relevant to child therapy. In general the mothers expected therapy to be a personal, somewhat non-directive experience for their child. Mothers also assumed that treatment would be shorter or would last for fewer sessions than estimated by the child's therapist. The expected duration of treatment is, thus, one issue that should be addressed and clarified in the early stages of therapy. The scheduling of sessions, the fees, and other parental responsibilities also need to be covered. Most importantly, the first session with the parents will ideally set the stage for the parents and therapist to work together for the best interests of the child.

Termination

Therapy does not last forever—it is an episode in a child's life. At some point the child and the therapist will say good-bye and therapy will terminate. Termination is an individual matter, and good-byes are said in many ways. Termination brings with it increased possibilities for regression as well as for growth, so it must be taken seriously and approached carefully. Although there are no "right" or "wrong" ways to terminate psychotherapy, a successful termination will help the child resume growth without the therapist.

Deciding to Terminate: There are no sure, precise guidelines for deciding when to end therapy. Termination is appropriate whenever the goals of therapy have been reached or when further progress is not possible. Therapy is not designed to handle all of a child's problems. It may be appropriate to terminate even though there are areas worthy of further consideration. At some point the child may benefit more from being on his or her own than from continuing to depend on the therapist. Ending need not await the child's becoming totally self-actualized or problem-free or fully functioning. Termination, instead, is usually a compromise along the way.

When working with children there are no absolute rules regarding the number of sessions needed. Treatment may vary from short-term emergency or brief psychotherapy to longer-term interventions. While experiential psychotherapy generally has no set time-limits, the average or modal length of treatment tends to be somewhere between 6 months and 1 ½ years. This form of treatment is, thus, typically shorter than traditional psychoanalysis and longer than emergency or brief psychotherapies. Within experiential psychotherapy the number of sessions ideally will depend on the rate of the client's growth. Other factors external to the process of therapy, such as families moving or terminating therapy for other reasons, may also affect the length of treatment. Therapists may consider the following factors when they determine how much time the client will need.

1. What is the quality of the child's family life? Is the family motivated, able, and willing to promote and sustain the child's improvement over an extended period? Factors such as family mobility, time schedules, and finances affect the length of treatment. External factors that facilitate a child's therapy make longer-term interventions more feasible, while external factors that disrupt therapy may result in briefer interventions or premature terminations.
2. Are the child's problems mild, recently developed, or caused by a stressful event? Children who are less disturbed or who are experiencing adjustment disorders may be amenable to briefer interventions, while seriously disturbed children with chronic problems typically require many sessions.
3. What are the child's strengths, and how has the child managed or adapted to stress in the past? Children who possess strengths as well as weaknesses may progress faster. A child's history of having adjusted to or "recovered" from previous difficulties can be useful information for estimating treatment length (Cooper and Wanerman 1977). Children who have bounced back quickly in the past are more likely to respond to briefer interventions, but those who have not demonstrated such resiliency will most likely require more time in therapy.

The decision to terminate ideally will be made jointly by the child, the parents, and the therapist. It is important to remember that these three parties usually have different objectives for therapy. Their reasons for wanting to terminate may also differ and should always be explored fully. When a therapist wishes to terminate a child's therapy, he or she should be certain of why. Is it because the child has progressed and grown and no longer requires the therapeutic relationship? If this is so, termination is appropriate and the child and parents should be told.

Whenever the child or the child's parents wish to terminate, the therapist should listen and try to understand. Ideally, termination will be brought up by the child rather than by the therapist. When the child comes to see therapy as a form of dependency which is no longer necessary, the therapy has succeeded and is ready to end.

Children and their parents, however, sometimes expect less from therapy than does the therapist. Some parents may be content with the relief of the child's symptoms. They may want to end a child's therapy just at the time the therapist thinks things are getting started or growth is beginning. As a general rule clients want to terminate therapy when they feel better. This may mean that the problem situation has been satisfactorily resolved, that they have learned better coping skills, or simply that external events have changed so that their stress is lessened (Zaro et al. 1977).

The client's desire to terminate is usually based on several factors. Progress made toward therapeutic goals certainly influences the client's decision. When the child and parents feel that their goals have been reached, it will seem appropriate to them to stop the therapy. There is a risk of premature termination when children and parents wish to avoid painful feelings stirred up by a child's therapy. Sometimes, especially in the beginning of a child's treatment, "improvement" may appear troublesome to the parents. A child's first attempts to relate differently or handle situations in new ways are not always met with parental approval. Wanting to terminate can also be related to practical matters such as difficulties with financing or scheduling a child's therapy. Parental motivation to continue a child's treatment may have limits if it poses other problems of difficulties for the family.

At times, clients want to terminate abruptly or prematurely. Therapists may avoid this by being alert to clues that the child or parents are thinking about quitting and by discussing the clues before the decision is final. Although the child or parents may not openly state their intentions to quit treatment, various remarks may be revealing. Statements such as, "I'm not sure we are doing the right thing" or, "Adam doesn't seem to be getting better." or, even more directly, "I'm wondering if therapy is helping." must be listened to and explored. At such moments the therapist should share his or her perceptions of a child's progress and relate them to the goals of therapy. Frequent lateness or missed appointments can show indirectly that a family is getting ready to end a child's therapy. These unspoken messages also need to be addressed and explored.

Ideally the child, parents, and therapist will come to a common agreement as to when to terminate. Whatever the circumstances surrounding termination, however, the child and the parents have the final decision, and it must be respected. The therapist should not make strong attempts to influence a family's decision to end a child's therapy unless he or she believes it is a mistake that could cause serious harm to the child.

How to Terminate: Terminations should be anticipated; in fact, the mechanisms for terminating therapy can be built into the very first session. An understanding is sometimes reached initially that no one will end the therapeutic relationship without at least one session to discuss it first. That way, neither the child nor the parents will call and say that the child is never coming in again; if this occurs, the therapist can remind the caller that they had agreed to confer before making a final decision.

Setting an end point is a part of therapy that ideally evolves from review sessions with the child and the parents. During these sessions one can take stock of the therapeutic process and review what has been accomplished. Then the therapist can tell the client, "Things seem to be getting a lot better; you don't seem to need help as much; I think we've accomplished most of what we'd hoped to accomplish." They can discuss the skills that the child and parents have acquired to deal with future difficulties. The therapist may be wise to warn that some relapse may occur and to anticipate problems that might arise after treatment. When these fundamental issues are covered, a consensus should emerge as to the appropriate time to terminate.

The ending point should be clear to all involved. A mutually understood anticipation of the ending of therapy is an important part of the treatment process. Generally, experiential psychotherapy is open-ended, and the ending point evolves during the therapy process. Occasionally, however, the length of therapy is limited from the beginning, when the therapist and the child agree to see each other for a few weeks or months with the understanding that the relationship would end at the end of that time. Some short-term planned interventions may also provide a brief treatment period of six to ten sessions followed by a waiting period of three to four months. During this waiting period the child and family may independently sort out their issues and progress, and they can consider whether they need to return for more help. Whenever there are time limits, it is essential that the child, the parents, and the therapist are all aware that they exist.

Regardless of the structure of therapy, the last session should not be allowed to arrive without some prior mention. When all parties involved anticipate the end of therapy, the therapist can then begin planning the last session to help make it a positive experience.

It is often helpful to allow two to four sessions to work through and accomplish the termination process. When termination seems to be a month or so in the future, the therapist might prepare the child by cutting the number of visits in half, perhaps from once a week to twice a month. This process helps to show whether it is truly appropriate to terminate. Gradually cutting therapy back gives the child an opportunity to practice getting along without therapy. It also exposes the child's ability to deal with environmental stresses that may present themselves over time. Other breaks in treatment can also help the child rehearse the ending. Vacations and illnesses may disrupt therapy and permit the child to assume responsibility without the help of the therapist. Perhaps a crisis can be prevented by not terminating abruptly and by providing the child and parents time to adjust to termination.

Some discussions about termination can help the child to clarify what therapy has accomplished and what the ending signifies. It is helpful for verbal children to talk about the therapeutic relationship and to put it into their own words. Encouraging a child to talk about the ending of therapy may better enable the child to accept it. Various questions may facilitate this process, for example, "How will it feel to stop coming here?" or, "What do we still need to do?" For less verbal children, play may facilitate communication about termination. A therapist working with a younger child might, for example, tell the child, "Draw a good-bye picture for me."

At times, therapy ends prematurely because of external conditions or causes. Parents may move, experience scheduling conflicts, or decide for an array of reasons that their child's therapy should be ended. Therapists themselves may need to terminate a child's treatment prematurely because of employment changes. Also, some public facilities and health plans restrict the number of sessions.

When external factors limit the length of treatment, therapy may still be appropriate and helpful even though growth may be limited (see the case study of Alex in Chapter 5). Perhaps with some support a family may also mobilize itself in other ways to structure any further needed care. Whenever treatment will be limited, it is essential that the limitations be clear to the child and the family. At these moments the therapist can acknowledge the restrictions and plan for a termination, knowing that only limited gain or goals may be realized.

At times therapy ends in failure. Sometimes a therapist cannot help a child. It is better to stop in failure than to continue with a relationship that is not able to help. One may need to acknowledge this. No therapist can be successful with all children. The therapist may have to convey the idea, "This doesn't seem to be working out; I don't think extending the number of sessions will help. I can't help, but maybe someone else could." The therapist may have to phrase this a bit more softly, but it is certainly a genuine, congruent reason to end therapy.

When therapy ends, children should understand that they are free to call back for additional services or consultation should serious problems arise. They should know that whenever they need help they can call the therapist's office and be received. The option of entering therapy again should be presented as a viable and acceptable possibility for the future. Termination should also not imply to children or their parents that the changes initiated by therapy will not continue. Following termination, children may well continue to improve and grow as critical changes produce positive results (Zaro et al. 1977).

Coordinating with Parents: Parents must be fully involved in the decision to terminate a child's treatment. When therapy ends, the child and the parents must resume functioning without assistance. Parents may have varied reactions to a child's treatment and its termination. Some parents approach therapy as a means of relief for their child's symptoms, and wish to end a child's therapy prematurely. Others may hope that a child's therapy will continue as long as possible because they are afraid of having to cope with the child after the safety of therapy is gone.

A satisfactory relationship with the parents will facilitate a child's therapy and its appropriate ending. Parents who can relate to the therapist about issues surrounding a child's therapy are better able to understand their child's needs and to recognize the child's (and perhaps their own) progress and growing capacity to manage without therapy.

When a child's therapy ends, it is important to consider whether the parents are able to resume parenting unaided. If a child is ending therapy and returning to effective parents, the child should flourish and progress. Perhaps, though, a child's therapy is only one part of what a family needs. Some parents may need to continue with individual therapy attending to their own problems and personal needs; others may need marital counseling or family therapy. When ending a child's therapy it is always important to reassess and tend to the child's environment. Additional services, if needed, should be recommended and made available.

Reactions to Termination: Certain reactions and feelings typically accompany the decision to end treatment. Children might be sad and reluctant to give up the unconditional valuing of an intimate therapeutic relationship. They may feel threatened or anxious about their ability to resolve problems independently and successfully in the future. The idea of termination may conjure up disturbing memories and feelings associated with separations from other important people. Terminations may also trigger more positive reactions. Children may feel relieved or happy or proud that they have successfully resolved a difficulty and can now function more independently. They can experience mastery or gain self-confidence from being able to say good-bye to the therapist.

Since it can be very difficult for children to give up such a rare and significant relationship, therapists must part with them carefully. Therapists must give children credit for being able to understand intellectually the need for therapy eventually to end, even though the children will probably not have the affective capacity to accept it. Therapists must use this conflict to therapeutic ends. They must be at the service of the children to help them weather this difficult experience, giving as much therapeutic support as possible.

At termination the child may exhibit a variety of behaviors (Adams 1974). Fear, anger, and aggression may be a child's way of trying to ease the pain of parting. The child who has just learned to control behavior problems may act them out again in therapy. In milder forms, a child may become bored or inattentive during therapy sessions. Such behaviors can reflect reactions to perceived rejection or attempts to control the pending separation. If so, the therapist might congruently say, "It seems hard to say good-bye."

Some relapsing of the child's initial problems may also reappear. The encopretic child may have another accident and the child who has trouble separating from Mother may once again not want to go to kindergarten. Such relapses, when closely tied to termination, can reflect a child's reluctance to let go. When relapsing is a child's bid to extend therapy, termination becomes the therapeutic issue.

Some children protest termination directly. A child may ask to continue or to come back "just one more time." A young child may want to take and keep a toy or other reminder of the therapist and therapy. Another child may want reassurance of the possibility of contact with the therapist. While a clear ending is best, it is acceptable to convey that a future contact would be allowed. Some reassurances may be needed to help the child say good-bye.

Therapists reactions to termination may include feelings of relief, anxiety, sadness, anger, and rejection. Therapists might have difficulty terminating with clients because of their own desire to nurture or to continue the therepeutic relationship. They may not want to separate from chidren with whom they have experienced close relationships. The rejection therapists feel when their clients want to end the relationship can easily contaminate their perception. Therapists must deal with such reactions; their needs must not interfere at the time of termination.

For therapists, termination often brings feelings of ambivalence. Work with children is satisfying and rewarding, especially when they grow and adapt as a result of their relationship. At the same time, sensitive therapists are often saddened when they and the clients with whom they have felt so much are parting.

5

Case Studies

Having reviewed the conditions necessary for therapeutic gain with children, we will now illustrate how these might express themselves in three cases. The best-known case study employing Rogerian methods with a child is *Dibbs, In Search of Self* (Axline 1964). That work should serve as useful background material for a better understanding of this section. Here, however, we will illustrate the more current principles of experiential psychotherapy.

Gee, Chris, and Alex represent real children who benefited from treatment. The portions of their therapy detailed here are intended to illustrate the integration of separate techniques into a single therapeutic dialogue.

Gee

(An early adolescent boy with difficulties in personality and character formation)

Gee was a 13-year-old seventh-grade student when he was first referred to a guidance center. He was described as uncooperative, uncontrollable, and antisocial. Such behavior also typified his early response to the psychotherapeutic setting. Gee was assigned to a male therapist in his early thirties who was told that Gee had a reputation for picking on younger children at school and was on the verge of being expelled.

Gee's family lived in a lower-middle-class neighborhood. His father worked for a very modest wage at a local rock quarry. Their diet included large amounts of day-old bread from a bargain bakery outlet, and powdered milk. Family members were frequently dressed in second-hand clothes, and little attention was paid to grooming. In general, the parents seemed poor but resourceful.

Both parents had dropped out of high school. Gee's mother appeared to be the dominant member of the family. His two younger sisters seemed to be developing in a reasonably uncomplicated fashion. The mother reported that her pregnancy and delivery with Gee were unremarkable, with one important exception: her husband was not Gee's biological father. (Some of the suspicions concerning Gee's nonbiological father's ineptness, lack of awareness, and passivity, were borne out in the subsequent observations of him.)

Gee was scheduled for one visit per week with his therapist. During the early sessions he was reluctant to choose an activity. In order to respect the principle of responsibility, the therapist waited comfortably for Gee to choose what to do or what to talk about, and eventually Gee would use a variety of materials during each session. He seemed, however, to resent having to help clean up the playroom. The therapist felt he would not be acting in Gee's best interest if he let himself be used as a busboy. Among other things, he thought that this might adversely affect the transference aspects of their relationship. On the other hand, the therapist sensed that after (and only after) an intimate relationship had been established, Gee's tendency to show transference by manipulating the therapist into a "use or be used" relationship might serve as a useful event. The goal would be for the therapist to point out, congruently, what he felt Gee was doing and to raise the issue of how this might typify Gee's ways of handling other interpersonal situations. To ensure that possibility, he made it a rule that all equipment would have to be returned to the correct storage place at the end of each session. Equipment not returned could not be used for future sessions.*

During the first session, Gee undertook an activity typically enjoyed by children younger than himself—playing with toy trucks in a sandbox. At the end of the session, he refused to return this equipment to the storage shelf, and was told that he would lose the privilege of playing with it in the next session.

In the second session, Gee showed no interest in the toy trucks, although he seemed cognizant of the limit relating to them. He finally decided to finger-paint. Not surprisingly, he also refused to assist the therapist in cleaning up the fingerpaints.

Therapist: Well, our time is about up [*First valuing Gee*]. I've really enjoyed

---

*This strategy underlines the importance of the therapist's congruence in neo-Rogerian or experiential psychotherapy. The therapist would not be honest with himself if he reinforced Gee's rule-bending behavior during the therapy hour. However, it also demonstrates how neo-Rogerian psychotherapy blends itself with both the learning (reinforcement) and the dynamic (transference) approaches. The experiential approach, by adding phenomenologic/existential ideas, thus expands upon efforts such as those of Dollard and Miller (1950), who combined learning theory and dynamic psychology into a single unified system.

painting with you today; I especially enjoyed showing you how a few things are painted, because you learn so fast. [*Then congruently*] But our time's up and we must put things away.

Gee: [*Says nothing, sits back in his chair with his arms folded*]

Therapist: [*Empathically, to nonverbal cues*] I sense that you enjoyed painting, too. [*Then, in an effort at intimacy*] It's sometimes more fun to enjoy something with another person. [*Then back to empathy*] But you seem to be telling me that you're through and don't intend to assist with the cleanup.

Gee: [*Looks the therapist in the eye, nods his head slowly in the affirmative*]

Therapist: [*Stressing responsibility*] That's okay. [*Then therapist congruence*] But I will have to add these painting materials to the list of things we won't play with in the future.

By the fifth session, Gee and the therapist had used up the remaining equipment in the therapy room. The only items not on the "no longer available" list were a few wooden blocks. These were made from 2″ × 4″ boards, and ranged from 4″ to 18″ in length. They could be used to build a variety of structures. Gee, apparently thinking ahead, got out all but one block. As anticipated, he refused to restore the blocks, which the therapist assured him was all right.

The therapist and Gee then entered the sixth therapy session with only one 18″ × 2″ × 4″ block available for play. Midway through the session Gee announced that he did not think the therapist was fair in taking away all the equipment.

Therapist: You seem angry, and you also seem frustrated when someone enforces a rule consistently.

Gee: [*Responds by swinging the 2″ × 4″ block into the wall, making a gash*]

Therapist: [*Shocked, yet still able to respond congruently*] I hope both of us know that I can't let you do that.

Gee: [*Starts to swing again*]

Therapist: [*Carefully grabbing the block away from Gee*] I'll have to have that.

Gee: I don't need the block. I can kick the wall, you know.

Therapist: I can't let you do that either. If you do, we'll have to move to a very small room with cement block walls.

Gee responded by kicking the wall, whereupon the therapist opened the door with one hand and grabbed Gee's wrist with the other. He then escorted Gee to a small cubicle that served as an observation room. Conveniently, it had tile floors and cinderblock walls.

After only a few minutes in the new room, Gee's approach changed considerably.

Gee: Can we go back to the old room for our next session if I promise not to tear it up?

Therapist: [Congruently] That question really surprises me, but I'm glad to hear you ask. I'll agree for us to go back as long as you don't damage anything. We could start with a few blocks, and if everything is put away at the end of the session, I'll bring out some new equipment for the next one.

Despite the extensive amount of limit setting that characterized the early stages of therapy, an intimate relationship seemed to evolve between the therapist and Gee. The therapist noted that physically removing Gee from the original therapy room coincided with a positive change in their relationship. The change seemed to have been heightened by the therapist's care to emphasize acceptance while enforcing limits. Apparently, Gee's need for structure and the therapist's ability to provide it in an atmosphere of warmth contributed much to the growing relationship.

At the beginning of the seventh session, the therapist and Gee walked arm in arm as they entered the old activity room.

Gee: [Apparently responding positively to being touched] You like me, don't you?

Therapist: Yes, I like you very much. And, I'm pleasantly surprised to hear you ask that. [Note that this response takes advantage of opportunities to value the client and to be congruent]

Gee: I think I've figured something out. The people you can play tricks on are the people who don't like you and the ones you can't play tricks on are the ones who do like you.

Therapist: That sounds insightful; I'm impressed.

Gee: Yeah, you're a tough cookie, just like some of my teachers. But I think you like me like some of them do.

Therapist: [Blending congruence, valuing, and responsibility] You're certainly right that I like you, and if being a tough cookie is in your best interest, then I'll be that way. I want very much to be of help to you. I wouldn't like to see anything bad happen to you. I don't want anything to happen that would keep you from being what you want to be most.

Gee: [Only smiles]

Therapist: [Empathically to nonverbal cue] That smile tells me that I was on the right track.

With the tenth session, Gee began to fingerpaint on a regular basis. During the twelfth session, he painted a catfish swimming on the bottom of a pond. The catfish was very black, and the water appeared murky. That, combined with Gee's general demeanor, indicated depression.

Therapist: [*Attempting empathy*] You seem to have a heavy feeling today.
Gee: Yeah. How'd you know?
Therapist: Just by seeing the way you acted and by looking at the picture you were drawing.
Gee: [*Continues to paint in silence*]
Therapist: [*Congruently*] I'd like to hear more about the heavy mood if you feel like telling me about it, but [*Preserving the principle of responsibility*] if you'd rather not talk about it, you know that's okay, too.
Gee: It's Mom. She hit me today. That always gives me a bad feeling.
Therapist: [*Continuing to be congruent, even somewhat aggressively so*] That makes me even more curious about what happened.
Gee: Well, she asked me if I was mad at her and I said I was, and she hit me.
Therapist: That sounds strange to me.
Gee: What's strange about it?
Therapist: I would have expected her to hit you for something you *did,* and you make it sound as if she hit you for some kind of *feeling* you had.
Gee: The worst thing you can do is let her know you're mad at her. She just goes bananas. She'll scream at you, or hit you, or both.
Therapist: That still seems unusual.
Gee: So, whoever said Mom isn't strange?
Therapist: Let me make sure I have this right. Your mom hit you, not because of anything you did, but because you were angry with her. How can she know whether or not you have a certain feeling?
Gee: Well, it was like this. She burned a hole in my favorite shirt when she was trying to iron it. I have only two shirts, and she ironed the one I like better in the same spot for so long that it burned a hole in it. Now I can't wear it any more. I have only one shirt, and it's not the one I like.
Therapist: [*Valuing*] Hmm, I hate it that you've got this problem, [*Then congruently*] but I'm still not clear on why you got hit.
Gee: Well, I said, "Way to go, Mom. The kids at school are already kidding me about having only two shirts, and now I have just one, and it's the one I don't like, *thanks to you!*"
Therapist: Is there more to the story?
Gee: Then she said, "Are you getting mad at me?" and I said, "Yes." And she said, "You know you'd better not get mad at me." She started holler-

ing a bunch of other stuff and saying she was going to hit me. I said, "Go ahead. It doesn't hurt anyway." So she hit me with a wooden spoon.

Therapist: Well, I can understand why you feel heavy today, but mainly I'm just sorry you have to feel badly. [*Then congruently*] And, I wonder if it isn't confusing.

Gee: Mom's not confusing; she's just a bitch.

Therapist: [*Empathically*] So, you're mad as well as sad?

Gee: Yeah. Wouldn't you be?

Therapist: Well, I hope you know that when you're here, it's okay to think or feel anything you want. It's just the *behavior* you have to control. [*Then jokingly*] Remember the other therapy room?

Gee: Yeah. You mean the prison cell?

[*Gee and the therapist laugh together*]

During the fifteenth session, Gee again chose to play with toys typically enjoyed by younger children. He used a boy puppet to stomp other puppets, focusing particularly on stomping the mother puppet.

Therapist: The boy seems to be angry with the grownups.

Gee: Yeah.

Therapist: [*Congruently*] It's my nature; I can't help but wonder why.

Gee: Because they're so stupid.

Therapist: [*Congruently*] I'm not sure what you're saying. Are they stupid because they're not intelligent or because they do things when they know better?

Gee: They're just stupid.

Therapist: You mean they aren't intelligent?

Gee: Yeah.

Therapist: [*Empathically*] Then if those [*Points to puppets*] were your parents and the boy puppet is you, the boy puppet is angry because he is smarter than the parents?

Gee: Could be. But he's really angry because the parents don't have any money. They don't have a nice house, or nice clothes, or a nice car.

Therapist: Then the boy is also angry because he has less than other kids?

Gee: Yeah.

Therapist: Because he feels as though he isn't as good as other people? [*Then realizing his mistake of involving self-esteem*] I really meant as *important* as other people.

Gee: [*Says nothing*]

Therapist: [*Empathically*] That must feel strange because sometimes he feels superior to his parents, and yet he feels inferior to his friends.
Gee: [*Pointing to the puppet*] This kid does.

In the seventeenth session, Gee took sand from the sandbox and mixed it with his fingerpaints, grinding it into the picture. He also took great delight in playing with a rubber dart gun, shooting it aggressively and boisterously at spots on the wall. For the eighteenth session, the therapist brought a plastic toy that could be punched. Gee punched it frequently and vigorously.

Gee's mother had participated in a support group made up of other mothers whose children were in individual psychotherapy. The group's final session was held the same day as Gee's eighteenth visit. At the suggestion of Gee's therapist, some time in the final mothers' group session was devoted to differentiating between children's thoughts and feelings, on the one hand, and their overt behavior, on the other. The parents' group leader suggested that they exercise minimal control over their children's thoughts and feelings, explaining in lay terms that trying to control feelings tends to encourage repression. The leader suggested that discipline might best be aimed at overt behavior. During this meeting, Gee's mother reported fewer problems with him at home, and no recent complaints from school personnel. Soon after the eighteenth session, Gee enrolled in a summer day camp and sports program provided by the city. His grooming seemed to be improving and he announced that he was now getting a haircut once a month. But just prior to the twenty-first session, a house in Gee's neighorhood was vandalized. The police and Gee's parents suspected him. The parents decided to ask the therapist to discuss this matter with Gee rather than do so themselves. The alternative was to have him interrogated directly by the police. The therapist discussed the matter with Gee in the following conversation.

Therapist: Before we begin today, there's something I want to talk over with you.
Gee: Okay.
Therapist: Your parents tell me a house in your neighborhood had a window broken out and some walls damaged. The police have told your parents that they have some evidence that you're the one who did it.
Gee: Well, I didn't.
Therapist: They asked me to talk with you to see if I could find out the facts rather than their doing it or having the police talk with you.
Gee: [*Angrily*] There's nothing to find out!
Therapist: You seem irritated by all this.
Gee: Wouldn't you be if you were always being accused of something?

Therapist: So you are angry because you're being accused of something you didn't do?

Gee: Right. You got it!

Therapist: Well, the police feel differently. They say that if you admit you did it you'll have a meeting with the court counselor, but you won't have to go to court, provided you pay for the damage. If you don't confess, they say there will be an inquiry and possibly a trial.

Gee: Why is everybody always picking on me? Are you going to let them do that?

Therapist: I can't interfere with the police doing their job, even if it involves you.

Gee: The easiest thing is to say I did it whether I did or not.

Therapist: You seem to feel trapped, even willing to admit a crime you didn't do in order to get out.

Gee: [*To the therapist's surprise*] No, I *did* do it!

Therapist: Well, I'm glad you could tell me that. This way it won't make the situation worse.

Gee: [*Teary*] What happens now?

Therapist: You seem scared.

Gee: Yes. What are they going to do to me?

Therapist: Well, I think there'll be a meeting with the court counselor, who'll explain that you have to pay for the house repairs, and that this is the last mistake of this kind you can make without being taken to court.

Gee: Are you going to be there?

Therapist: Do you want me to come?

Gee: No, I'd rather you didn't come. I'd rather go by myself.

Therapist: You want to take the responsibility?

Gee: Right. I hope my parents don't blab about this to anyone else.

Therapist: I'm curious if you've asked them not to tell anyone else about this.

Gee: I'm going to tell them not to tell anybody. They'll say okay; then I'll see if they really do what they say they'll do.

In the twenty-second session, Gee chose to spend an entire session playing in the sandbox, although this activity seemed somewhat unusual for a boy of his age. He worked with the sand in a rather sophisticated fashion, taking the entire hour to construct an elaborate sand castle town. In the middle of the town was one structure considerably higher than the others.

Therapist: That one building looks different from the others.

Gee: It's City Hall.

Therapist: That's interesting. I'm curious about what goes on there.

Gee: The mayor and the lieutenant mayor work there. You're the mayor and I'm the lieutenant mayor.

Therapist: [*Smiling so as to indicate that he's joking*] Sounds like Batman and Robin.

Gee: Yeah. Sometimes I play games with my soldiers, and you're the general and I'm the lieutenant. We always win.

Therapist: [*Empathically*] It sounds like you wish I were your leader, and you were following in my footsteps.

Gee: Yeah.

Therapist: You seem to feel stronger if there's someone who cares about you whom you can follow.

Gee: Yeah.

The first day of eighth grade for Gee coincided with the twenty-fourth session. Gee and his eighth-grade homeroom teacher appeared to be a fortunate match. Gee made high grades in that teacher's class (math) and seemed to be particularly impressed by the fact that the teacher had played golf for his college golf team. The teacher in return seemed to like Gee and responded positively to his budding athletic skills. Gee was becoming known as a good softball and soccer player, and was playing on the junior high football team.

In the thirtieth session, Gee described a situation in which he'd been asked to join a social club at school for which eighth- and ninth-grade boys were eligible.

Gee: I've been asked to join the Brigadiers. It's a guys' club, but they're not the best guys. I told Waylon, the guy who asked me, that I wanted to wait and join the Cavaliers. Their guys are better.

Gee was not invited to join the Cavaliers. A fellow student teased him about turning down one social club so he could join another, then not being invited into the second. This angered Gee to the point that he hit the student. He was sent to the principal's office but was not placed on probation. Gee recounted these experiences in the thirty-fourth session.

Therapist: [*Empathically*] It really makes you angry when someone takes advantage of you when you're down.

Gee: Yeah.

Therapist: It sounds like it reminds you of some other experiences.

Gee: What do you mean?

Therapist: Like when some of the kids made fun of you for having only two shirts.

Gee: Yeah, but I'm going to show them. I'm going to be the best football player there is, and I'm going to get a good job, and someday I'm going to make a lot of money.

Around the thirty-fifth session Gee's behavior took on a decidedly intellectual flavor. He noticed a set of encyclopedias in the waiting room and began bringing one into the therapy session. Gee and the therapist often played a game in which Gee would ask questions on a topic covered by the encyclopedia. These were usually questions the therapist could not answer. When the therapist failed, Gee would read or paraphrase the answer from the book, taking great delight in "teaching" the therapist. Subsequent sessions showed that Gee was retaining a great deal of the material that he had taught the therapist.

On the thirty-ninth session, Gee brought some carrot sticks, celery, and radishes wrapped neatly in plastic wrap. He offered a vegetable to the therapist and took one himself.

Therapist: Your bringing me these vegetable sticks reminds me of our early sessions.
Gee: How's that?
Therapist: Well, we used to begin by going to the snack bar for graham crackers or granola bars. It's like I used to be the one feeding you, but now you're the one feeding me.
Gee: Yeah. It's okay, isn't it?
Therapist: Yes, but I think I see a message in what you're doing.
Gee: What's that?
Therapist: It's like you're starting to think about taking care of someone else instead of being taken care of.
Gee: I can take care of myself now.
Therapist: That makes me wonder if it's time to think about ending our sessions. Maybe you don't need to come in any more.
Gee: I've thought about that.
Therapist: Well, we could handle it in a couple of different ways. If you're sure you're ready to stop coming in, we can just stop. Or if you'd like to come in less frequently, like every other week, we could do that.
Gee: What do you think I should do?
Therapist: I think you should do what you feel is best for you.
Gee: Maybe we could have one or two more sessions.
Therapist: That's fine with me. Why don't we plan to have a couple more, and we'll discuss when to stop as we go along.

During the next (fortieth) session, Gee indicated that he had thought about termination and had decided that this should be his last session. The therapist agreed. He then asked Gee what he'd like to do in the way of activities. Gee began to tinker with a baby buggy that was stored in the corner of the activity room. Gee proceeded to put a number of puppets into the buggy, and to wheel it about the room. He took his puppet family to a ball game, where, like a dutiful father, he explained meticulously everything that was going on in the field of play. Finally, near the end of the session:

> *Gee:* I have something I'd like to do.
> *Therapist:* What's that?
> *Gee:* See if I can push you in the baby buggy.
> *Therapist:* I'm willing to try.

The therapist sank cautiously into the baby buggy, which Gee then moved around the room for a couple of turns. When he stopped, the therapist struggled to extricate himself from the buggy.

> *Therapist:* To me, this says you're not a kid any more. Not only are you able to take care of yourself, but you're well on your way to being able to care for others. I really enjoy our relationship. I wish you the very best. And remember, I'll be here, should you want to be in touch.
> *Gee:* [*Confidently*] I'll be in touch.

The therapist received a Christmas card from Gee during each of the next three years. At last report Gee was a regular on the high school's cross-country team, was doing well in his classes, and was staying out of trouble.

Chris

(An 8-year-old girl with psychosomatic difficulties)

Chris was referred to a child guidance clinic by her family physician because of gastrointestinal problems including hyperacidity, spasms, and vomiting. Recent episodes had become more intense. Chris had been hospitalized for three weeks for treatment and testing, but no physical causes could be identified. Upon referral, Chris was back at home with continuing gastrointestinal disturbance. Reportedly she was vomiting several times daily. Chris had lost ten pounds in the past two months and frequently complained of poor appetite, sleep disturbance, and dizziness. Medication seemed to provide her with some relief. Chris's family physician had first prescribed a regime of antacids and smooth muscle relaxants, then referred her to the child guidance clinic to determine the role of psychogenic forces in her stomach disturbance, and to decide whether psychotherapy would be useful.

For the initial interview the therapist met with Chris and her parents. Chris was pale and sat somewhat reclined, covering herself with a coat throughout the session. She was soft-spoken, and appeared tired, slow-moving, and rather expressionless. When the topic of school was introduced, Chris conveyed that she was feeling sick.

> *Chris:* I think I'm going to be sick. I may throw up.
> *Therapist:* [*Valuing*] I'm sorry that you are not feeling well. Let me show you where our restroom is. [*Therapist and Chris leave the therapy room*]
> *Therapist:* Can I get you anything?
> *Chris:* I don't think so.
> *Therapist:* [*Expressing empathy but giving Chris the responsibility for managing the situation*] Please let me know if I can do anything for you, otherwise, I'll return and visit further with your parents.
> *Chris:* I'll be okay. I just need to stay here awhile. I may throw up.
> *Therapist:* [*Begins to depart*] Let me know if you need anything, and join us when you feel better.

The therapist returned alone to the therapy room and resumed the interview with the parents. Several minutes later Chris returned without comment and took her place in the room.

During the initial interview the family wanted to talk about Chris's medical difficulties. They had been surprised to find out that all medical tests were negative and that Chris might have emotional problems. They had felt that the vomiting was attributable to a food allergy. Both Chris and her family also expressed concern about problems with school. Chris, a third grader, reported academic difficulties as well as problems in relating to her teachers. These difficulties apparently dated back to kindergarten. At the time of referral to the guidance clinic, Chris was making satisfactory grades, but at times she reportedly worked very hard on assignments only to get unsatisfactory marks. Chris was unable to identify a favorite subject or special activity that she enjoyed at school. She also appeared to have some difficulty in relating to peers. She had not attended school for the past two months and was receiving instruction at home.

Chris lived with her parents, a younger brother, and an older sister. Her father was an engineer and her mother a homemaker. Chris's siblings were reportedly doing "just fine." Chris's parents also acknowledged that she was not relating well to her brother and sister. In response, Chris said that her brother and sister were too noisy and that they bothered her. Chris seemed closest to her mother. The mother, in turn, appeared to be particularly sensitive to Chris's needs, while the father seemed more passive and withdrawn.

According to the parents' report, Chris's developmental history was relatively normal. She did have some apparent difficulties with gross motor development and was described as a clumsy child. Her medical history also included several head injuries. The most serious of these was a concussion that she sustained two years before in a car accident.

The parents reported that they had no idea as to what could be bothering Chris. They indicated that she did not seem to be worried about anything in particular. To the therapist, however, she seemed to be struggling with several concerns, including school achievement and problems in relating to both adults and peers.

At the conclusion of the initial interview the therapist advised the family that Chris could benefit from psychotherapy; she also recommended additional testing to obtain a more complete developmental/psychological picture. The parents agreed to proceed, and Chris was referred to both psychological and neurological testing. The psychological evaluation suggested that Chris was mildly depressed and concerned about her ability to cope with various situations. Her self-esteem seemed quite low, and her dependency on her mother seemed high. Intellectually she was functioning within the low normal range of intelligence. The pattern was consistent with that of a mild, visual motor learning disability. The neurological assessment revealed clumsiness and difficulty with laterality, hopping, and tandem walking, which was also consistent with a diagnosis of learning disability. Her EEG was normal.

Chris's treatment plan included individual therapy for her and separate collateral sessions for her parents. All seemed quite willing to come in for the recommended sessions. Additional contact with Chris's teachers was also planned in order to share information concerning her personal problems and learning difficulties.

The therapist also shared with the parents her belief that it would be useful for Chris to have support from others and the opportunity to work toward her own solutions to her problems. They were encouraged to support Chris's development of autonomy and to minimize their special treatment of her.

Chris was brought to her first therapy session by her mother. They arrived twenty minutes early. Chris entered the playroom quietly and slowly. She found a chair by a low table and sat down:

Therapist: This is your hour to do with as you please. There are games and toys that you may choose to play with. We can also just talk or sit if you wish.

Chris: [*No comment. Continues to sit very still and occasionally glances hesitantly around the room*]

Therapist: [*2–3 minutes later*] You look as if you are not quite sure what to do.

Chris: What do *you* think we should do?

Therapist: [*Conveying responsibility*] I think that while we are here together that it's up to you to decide what to do.

Chris: [*No comment. Continues to sit and looks mildly uncomfortable*]

Therapist: [*2 minutes later. Therapist observes empathically*] It seems to be hard for you to decide what you want to do.

Chris: Yeah, well. [*Looks around and sees some crayons and paper on a shelf nearby*] Do you like to color?

Therapist: Yes. Can we get the crayons and paper down?

Chris: Okay.

The therapist and Chris then proceeded to color. Chris drew slowly and meticulously. She frequently asked for directions regarding drawing. Her coloring was somewhat laborious, and some perceptual motor difficulties were apparent. After coloring, Chris shifted more readily to other activities in the playroom. Yet, her play was still restricted and she often hesitated when approaching toys. She would frequently look to the therapist for direction and approval. When the time for the session was up, Chris politely left.

Chris's early play sessions were characterized by her hesitancy to direct the therapy session and her dependent style of relating to the therapist. Throughout the early sessions she looked to the therapist for direction and approval. The therapist continued to leave the responsibility for structuring the sessions to Chris. However, the therapist sometimes found it difficult to avoid being drawn into taking responsibility for the activity of the therapy session. During these early sessions, Chris also did not feel well, and her affect was somewhat depressed. She preferred less active toys and games and spent most of the session sitting in a chair. Her play and verbal interactions were restricted and inhibited. An excerpt from Chris's third session illustrates her quiet play as well as her preoccupation with her health. During this session Chris elected to play with a stuffed animal. She selected a stuffed puppy, which was one of her favorite toys, and a blanket and brought them both back to her chair:

Chris: He's cute. [*Wraps the puppy in the blanket and holds it. Sits holding the puppy and pats it occasionally*] Puppy's feeling sick.

Therapist: Oh, that's too bad. The puppy isn't feeling well.

Chris: Yeah. He's feeling sick and nobody knows why.

Therapist: It must be scary to feel sick when nobody knows why.

Chris: Yes. We need to take care of puppy. [*Continues to hold the puppy, petting and rocking it*]

Chris continued to play with and care for the puppy for some time. For the remainder of this session she played primarily with the stuffed animals and dolls. With these other toys she also adopted the role of a nurturing, concerned, overprotective mother. Chris seemed to experience some comforting as she cared for the toys.

By the eighth session Chris's gastrointestinal disturbance was showing improvement. At this point Chris was reportedly vomiting only occasionally and was experiencing only infrequent and mild stomach pain. Her psychosomatic difficulties appeared to respond rapidly to treatment, and initial improvements were noted first in this area. Chris was no longer getting sick during sessions and seemed to be defining herself less as an invalid. Chris's parents were extremely pleased with her progress.

For her tenth session Chris readily entered the playroom. As soon as she entered the room she gave the therapist a present:

Chris: I brought you a present. [*Hands the therapist a pen covered with a soft, furry fabric*]
Therapist: Oh! It's lovely. [*Examines pen*]
Chris: I made it for you.
Therapist: [*Valuing*] Well, then it's an extra special pen. I'll enjoy using it and thinking of you. Thank you very much.
Chris: What should we do today?
Therapist: [*Leaving the responsibility to Chris*] What would you like to do?
Chris: Could we color?
Therapist: Sure. Let's get the crayons and paper. I'll use my new pen.

Chris's present seemed to indicate a growing intimacy in the therapeutic relationship. While she seemed uncomfortable directing her actions during therapy, she did seem to feel increasingly comfortable with the therapist. Chris also appeared to value her sessions. This was conveyed throughout the remainder of her therapy sessions by her good attendance record, her promptness for sessions, and her occasional small handmade presents for the therapist.

By the thirteenth session Chris's play was becoming more self-initiated. The therapist also noted some oppositional tendencies in her play. Chris entered the playroom and went immediately to the doll house:

Chris: Let's play house. I'll be the baby. [*Plays with the dolls for several minutes*] Let's put them to bed. No. [*Holding the mama doll*] The mama doll tells the baby doll it's time to go to bed. It's time to go to bed. Look. [*Points to baby doll*] He won't go to bed. He doesn't want to. He says no. [*Smile*] He wants to stay up late and play.

Therapist: The mama wants the baby to go to bed but the baby doesn't want to.

Chris: Yeah. He stays up and plays and it's late. This baby gets to do whatever he wants to. [*Smiles*]

Therapist: The baby thinks it's fun to do whatever he wants to.

Chris: Yeah. He's going to have fun. He's going to eat candy, too. Now it's time to put the baby to bed. Let's put them to bed. [*Puts the dolls to bed. Pats the baby doll. Waits quietly a minute*] Now, it's morning. Good morning. [*Continues playing with the dolls*]

Throughout the remainder of this session Chris was more directive with her play. She more readily initiated activities and her play was more spontaneous.

Chris's play continued to be more self-directed. During the fifteenth session there were oppositional and aggressive tendencies in her play activities. She again chose to play with the stuffed animals and dolls, but this time her interactions were different. At one point during this session Chris chose her favorite stuffed puppy:

Chris: Puppy needs to get dressed. [*Goes over to the doll section of the playroom to get a dress, then puts it on the puppy*] There, that's better. [*Holds puppy and plays with it. Then looks at it*] Puppy's been bad. [*Frowns*] He scratched me. Bad puppy. [*Hits the puppy*]

Therapist: The puppy scratched you and that makes you angry.

Chris: Yes. He shouldn't do that. Let's put him up. [*Puts the puppy down under the toy bin. Walks around the playroom. Settles down with the playhouse. Picks up the baby*] The baby is thirsty. I'll give her some Kool Aid. [*Holds the baby and feeds the baby with a baby bottle*] This baby is named Mary Jane today. Where's the mama? And the daddy? Here they are. Where's her brother? Here he is. Okay. Let's see. I know. They are going to have dinner. And the mama fixed spinach and no one wants to come. Yuck. Spinach. [*Makes a face*] So they don't want to eat it.

Therapist: The family doesn't like spinach and doesn't want to eat it.

Chris: But the mama says that's what we're having for dinner—and they don't like it.

Therapist: Sometimes it makes us feel angry when others expect us to do things that we don't want to do.

Chris: Yeah, well. He's [*Baby*] going to fix chicken instead. [*Continues playing. Cooks dinner*]

Following the seventeenth session the therapist received a telephone call from Chris's mother. She was angry and concerned about Chris. She reported that Chris had recently refused to attend a family reunion. An argument had followed and Chris had stalked off to her room. The parents had decided to go on to the reunion and had left Chris at home with her older sister. Chris, in turn, was grounded for one week and not permitted to watch television. When the parents returned they found that a valuable dish had been broken. Chris denied breaking it, but her mother felt that she had broken it purposely. The therapist talked with Chris's mother over the phone and then recommended that she and her husband come in for a session to discuss their concerns with their own therapist.

During the parents' follow-up session the mother again reported her concerns to their therapist:

Mother: I'm really frustrated and angry with Chris. That family reunion was important to me and I really wanted her to attend. And breaking that dish that she knew I really liked . . . I don't know what's come over her. I don't know if she's making any progress. As a matter of fact, right now I feel that she's getting worse.

Therapist: I can see that you're angry and also concerned about the direction in which things are heading.

Mother: Yes. Chris and I aren't getting along the way we used to.

Therapist: [*Empathically*] It must feel bad not to be getting along with Chris. [*Then congruently*] But I must tell you that I believe that Chris *is* making progress. I have talked with Chris's therapist and she says that Chris is showing some improvement.

Mother: [*Pauses and demeanor softens*] Well, if I go back to the beginning, she was very sick and we didn't know what was wrong with her. She was vomiting all the time and we couldn't seem to help her. I was *really* worried about her then . . . and her health. Maybe she is better. I'd rather have her misbehaving than sick. [*Pause*] But right now is hard, too. I miss my nice little girl. Do you think that this too will get better?

Therapist: Actually, I do. Chris is learning to express herself, and since that's new for her she's sometimes awkward about it. Right now she seems to be doing it in a way that's troublesome for you and others. Over time though, Chris can learn to express herself more appropriately.

Mother: Well—it's some relief to hear that, but in the meantime, what do I do? How should we handle Chris?

Therapist: [*Congruently*] How about letting her practice expressing feelings with you? Perhaps if you could let her practice, she will get better at it. Could you let her express even her angry feelings?

Mother: Should I let her break things?

Therapist: No, I feel she needs limits, too. She needs to know that it's okay to feel angry and to let others know about it, but that it's not okay to break things.

Mother: Good.

Therapist: I also sense that you've been reevaluating the wisdom of Chris's continuing in therapy. I feel it would be helpful if we talked about that, as well as about how to set limits without stifling the expression of her feelings.

After an extended discussion of the two preceding topics:

Therapist: Chris's therapist has recommended that her therapy continue so that she can get more help in dealing with these issues.

Mother: [*Smiles*] Yesterday I was considering not bringing Chris back anymore. I was so angry. Maybe we just have some more work to do.

Following the parents' session, Chris arrived for her eighteenth session. She entered the therapy room quietly and picked up the toy puppy:

Therapist: You look as though you don't feel well today.

Chris: Yeah. I got in trouble at home. My Mom got real mad at me.

Therapist: I know. Your mother discussed with me some of the problems that you two were having.

Chris: Well, I didn't want to go to the reunion. I wanted to stay at home and watch a special TV show. And, besides, at reunions it's just grownup's talk and it's not fun.

Therapist: So you had a conflict between what you wanted to do and what your mom wanted you to do.

Chris: Yeah. We yelled at each other, and everybody felt bad, and I didn't even get to watch the TV program I wanted.

Therapist: [*Congruently*] I'm sorry that you felt bad, but I believe it's okay to feel angry sometimes.

Chris: [*Pause*] If I tell you something, will you not tell?

Therapist: Yes, of course.

Chris: I broke one of Mom's dishes. I didn't tell her that I did, but she thinks I did. I felt bad.

Therapist: [*Empathically*] You seem to feel guilty.

Chris: Yeah.

Therapist: You seem glad that you were able to tell your mother that you didn't want to go to the reunion and to let her know that you were angry.

But you seem to feel guilty about breaking the dish. Maybe the next time you can share those feelings without breaking things.

Chris: [*Does not comment, but continues playing*]

The start of Chris's fourth grade school term was scheduled to occur between her twenty-first and twenty-second sessions. In preparation for her return, a report regarding Chris was forwarded to her school. She was to be placed in a learning disability class for a portion of the day. Her teachers seemed supportive and willing to work with her to facilitate her transition back to the classroom.

During the twenty-first session Chris seemed somewhat preoccupied. She moved from toy to toy more rapidly than usual:

Chris: School is about to start and I'm going to be a fourth grader.

Therapist: I know.

Chris: It's going to be funny to be back in school again. I hope I do okay in school this year.

Therapist: It sounds like you're a little anxious about starting back to school.

Chris: Yeah. Sometimes it's really hard to do all the things they want you to do. And sometimes I can't do things as well as some of the other kids—then I feel bad.

Therapist: When you say "bad," do you mean like not very smart?

Chris: Yeah.

Therapist: Well, *I* know that you're not dumb.

Chris: [*Smiles but doesn't comment further*]

Chris's first day back at school went well. During her twenty-second session she reported that her new teacher was nice and that she hadn't gotten sick at school. Chris's adjustment during the next several weeks was positive and her grades were higher than the year before. In general, she seemed more relaxed regarding both achievement and interpersonal contacts. She reported minimal problems with stomach pains and nausea.

Around the twenty-fifth session Chris decided to make up a play for the therapist. Her performance was creative and clearly demonstrated her emerging capacity to structure and direct her activities. She asked the therapist not to watch while she practiced. After several minutes of rehearsal, Chris was ready to perform:

Chris: Okay. You can look now. This is a circus play. [*Holds a ball and uses it like a microphone*] Good evening ladies and gentlemen. First we have a performance from our Wonder Dog. [*Gets her favorite puppy and has it perform a series of tricks such as somersaults and flips*] Now Wonder Dog is done. [*Bows with Wonder Dog*]

Therapist: [*Applauds*]

Chris: Next we have an act called the horsey and the princess. [*Introduces a stuffed horse*] I'm going to be the princess and this is the horsey. [*Puts the horse on the floor. Jumps back and forth over the horse several times. Picks up the horse and pretends to ride it around*] I'm thinking how to ride this horse so he won't buck me off . . . I'm getting tired of this horsey. Come and help me. Put this horsey on my back. [*Therapist puts the horse on Chris's back*] I'm going to be the horsey. [*Crawls around on her hands and knees with the toy horse on her back, then bucks the horse off*] Let's see. I have another act. I haven't practiced this one yet . . .

Chris continued with several additional performances. She seemed to enjoy making up the acts.

By the twenty-eighth session, Chris had become interested in more interactive games. She selected some board games and card games to play with the therapist. Chris also began intermittantly mentioning Stacey, a girl friend at school.

By Chris's thirty-third session her physical and psychological status had improved to the point that the therapist raised the possibility of termination. Chris and the therapist were engaged in playing a board game called "Chutes and Ladders."

Chris: This is fun!

Therapist: You seem to be feeling good today.

Chris: MmHm. And I think I'm going to land on the big ladder.

Therapist: You know, I've been noticing that you seem to be feeling quite a bit better these days.

Chris: MmHm. I'm glad, too.

Therapist: I'm wondering if you may be feeling good enough that sometime soon we won't need to keep meeting.

Chris: Maybe so. But this is fun. It's my turn. [*Continues playing*]

On the thirty-fourth session Chris and the therapist talked again about the possibility of termination. They decided that they would meet every other week for a few more times and see how things went. The therapist also told Chris that they should discuss this new arrangement with Chris's parents. Chris, her parents, and the therapist met and all concurred that things were going well enough to end treatment.

Two weeks later Chris came in for her thirty-fifth session, and then two weeks after that she had her thirty-sixth and final session. She brought a picture that she had drawn of herself and the therapist. She had drawn herself lying down on a bed with one arm over her stomach and the therapist sitting in a chair beside her:

> *Chris:* This is for you. It's a picture of you and me. [*Points to the picture of herself*] That's when I wasn't feeling good.
> *Therapist:* It's a great picture. Thank you. [*Looks at the picture*] You were feeling bad then, weren't you? I'm glad that you're feeling better these days.
> *Chris:* Me, too. Can I come back to see you sometime if I don't feel good, or if I want to?
> *Therapist:* Sure. You can come back if you need to or if you just want to.
> *Chris:* Let's do something special today.
> *Therapist:* Okay. What would be special?
> *Chris:* Let's take a walk. Could we go to the pond and see the ducks? That would be fun.
> *Therapist:* Sure. That sounds like a great idea.

Chris's final session was, thus, spent taking a walk to a nearby pond. She seemed ready to say good-bye but did say that she would miss her sessions.

A followup report six months after termination indicated that Chris was adjusting to school and had not had recurrences of her gastrointestinal difficulties. While she continued to be somewhat shy, she was interacting more with both family members and peers.

Alex

(A 5-year-old boy with bruxism and behavior problems)

Alex was referred to a mental health service because of his aggressive behavior in his kindergarten classroom. Recently he had struck a child on the nose hard enough to make the child require medical attention, and on another occasion he had kicked his teacher. Alex's parents had been told that if his behavior did not improve soon he would not be allowed to continue with his current school placement.

In addition, Alex had a serious problem with tooth grinding (bruxism). He ground both front and jaw teeth, while awake and in his sleep. His front teeth were most profoundly affected, being ground almost to the gums. While Alex's grinding noises were at least minimally irritating to his parents and teachers, the greatest concern was for his dental health. If this behavior were not altered before permanent teeth erupted, Alex was destined to experience the negative dental and social consequences associated with the permanent loss of his front teeth.

Alex's parents felt they had relatively few problems with him at home. They thought that perhaps the school was not strict enough with him. They were concerned about his tooth grinding, but had been at a loss to know what could be done about it. They had consulted a dentist, who had warned of serious consequences but had prescribed nothing beyond advising them to get him to stop.

Alex was an attractive youngster somewhat large for his age. His parents reported that his early development was within normal limits. His teacher described him as a bright child who did well with academic tasks. Alex was an only child.

Alex's father was an active-duty military officer and his mother a home-maker. The family had moved often. Both parents reported that they were strict with Alex. They also revealed that their own upbringing had been strict. The parents reported some fighting amongst themselves, and said that they occa-sionally struck one another and that they had discussed divorce on several occasions. At the time of the referral, their relationship seemed benign, but distant.

Alex's parents were encouraged by a counselor to seek psychotherapeutic assistance for their marriage and for their child-rearing practices. They were polite but firm in their refusal to follow this suggestion. They did agree to let Alex see a therapist and to let the therapist provide consultation to Alex's teacher in order to facilitate Alex's adjustment to kindergarten.

During the first moments of Alex's first therapy session, the therapist seated himself in a chair against one wall of the small (approximately 10' × 10') playroom. Alex began by walking slowly and very methodically in circles about the room. At first the circles were very small. Gradually they increased in size and Alex began to observe the various toys located near the periphery of the room. With each pass he came closer and closer to the therapist, but did not look directly at him. The noise of grinding teeth was audible not only to the therapist but to observers in an adjoining booth. After several circles around the room, Alex finally passed within one or two feet of the therapist. At this point, the therapist reached out, picked Alex up and held him closely in his arms. Neither the therapist nor Alex said anything for approximately 10 minutes, but Alex tended to cling in a somewhat frightened manner.

[*After 10 to 15 minutes*]
Therapist: [*Empathically*] You seem scared.

Alex: [*Says nothing*]
Therapist: [*Congruently*] I can't really tell whether you're afraid of me or of something else.
Alex: [*Still says nothing*]

[*Although Alex did not respond verbally, his muscles seemed to relax and he clung less*]

Therapist: You seem to be feeling a little better now.
Alex: [*Still says nothing*]

At this point the therapist felt that there had been sufficient verbalization of empathy and decided to concentrate on greater intimacy. This he did by holding Alex gently and rocking him soothingly. Alex progressively loosened his grip on the therapist. By the end of the session, the therapist was holding Alex loosely and bouncing him gently on his knee.

Therapist: [*Valuing*] I've really enjoyed seeing you today and holding you. [*Then, congruently*] I think I enjoyed bouncing you the most, because somehow that says something good is happening to both of us. I'm looking forward to seeing you again, and maybe I can bounce you around more or even throw you up in the air next time.

It was at this point that Alex made his most dramatic communication of the day, a smile. The therapist also realized that Alex's tooth grinding noises had diminished steadily during the course of the session.

At the beginning of the second session, Alex and the therapist entered the room, and the therapist immediately took the same seat he had taken previously. Alex followed him to the chair, crawled up on his lap, and sat on his leg without hesitation. The therapist bounced Alex on his knee rather vigorously.

Therapist: [*Valuing*] I'm glad to see you today [*Then, empathically*] and you seem glad to see me [*Then, congruently*] and that makes me happy.
Alex: [*Smiles, but still says nothing. He does* not *grind his teeth*]

The therapist continued to bounce Alex, then initiated a game of pretending that Alex would fall, but catching him. This activity is a variation of the nursery rhyme game, "Ride the little horsey to market town; don't let the horsey fall down." Alex smiled more freely and even laughed out loud on a few occasions when he almost "bucked off" of the therapist's knee. Eventually the therapist, feeling that the "horsey" game had become redundant, suggested an alternative.

Therapist: How would you like for me to throw you up in the air?
Alex: [*Smiles and nods yes*]

The therapist stood behind Alex, grabbed him under the arms and tossed him into the air a few times.

Alex responded with laughter which became more gleeful as the tossing continued. Although he ground his teeth during the latter stages of this session, he did it considerably less than he had during the first session.

Between the second and third sessions the therapist talked with Alex's kindergarten teacher. The teacher reiterated her concerns for Alex but seemed relieved that his parents were letting Alex receive treatment. During this consultation the therapist shared his understanding of Alex and discussed the conditions that would facilitate his growth and adjustment. Alex's teacher appeared anxious to help the boy.

Upon entering the room for the third session, to the therapist's surprise, Alex began the conversation.

Alex: Throw me up in the air.
Therapist: [*The therapist responds by grabbing Alex under the arms and tossing him into the air*]

Alex seemed to enjoy the tosses, and after a while he raised his feet as the therapist lifted him, putting them above his head and attempting to touch the ceiling with his toes.

Therapist: You're getting to be quite an acrobat, almost like somebody in the circus. [*Then, empathically*] I can tell that you're getting less and less afraid that I might drop you. It seems that you're enjoying this more and that you're trying to become a better acrobat.
Alex: [*Smiling and straining harder to reach the ceiling with his toes*]

During this session Alex ground his teeth even less than he had before.

In the fourth session, Alex again entered and immediately asked to be thrown in the air. The therapist tossed Alex, and then made a congruent statement.

Therapist: Being thrown up into the air is something you seem to enjoy and something you are sure of between us. I wonder what would happen if I didn't throw you up in the air and you had to figure out something else to do.
Alex: [*Making no particular response to the therapist's statement, perhaps because it is over his head*]

After a few minutes of tossing, both the therapist and Alex sat down to catch their breath. Then they stared at each other, apparently thinking about what to do next.

> *Therapist:* [*Congruently*] You seem to be wondering what we're going to do next and looking at me to decide. I'm wondering the same thing and I'm looking to you to decide. [*Then, in a combination of congruence and limit setting*] I'm going to decide that when it isn't clear what we're going to do, you will decide what you would like to do and I'll follow you.

Alex looks somewhat nervous and confused. He walks about the room, inspecting the toys and grinding his teeth for the first time this session.

> *Therapist:* [*Empathically*] Having to decide what to do seems to make you nervous. [*Then, congruently*] I like you a lot, and I hate to see you nervous. [*Then, reinforcing the principal of responsibility*] However, I think it's best for you if you learn to make some decisions. Then making decisions should become easier for you.

Alex continued to pace and eventually selected a plastic inflatable toy with pictures of Batman and Robin on it. He pulled the toy to the center of the room where he began to use it as a punching bag. The therapist joined in, alternating strikes with Alex. Alex continued to hit the toy vigorously, but appeared to be more relaxed as he did so.

> *Therapist:* You're hitting the toy harder, but you seem to be letting something go rather than having something build up inside of you.
> *Alex:* [*Smiles broadly, begins hitting the toy less frequently and with less vigor*]

Alex was 25 minutes late for his fifth session. Much of the session was spent in hitting the Batman punching bag. He ground his teeth very little. The therapist terminated the session 5 minutes early so as to speak to Alex's mother. Upon entering the waiting room, he found the mother sitting alone.

> *Therapist:* I am sorry that Alex was late today. I'm not sure if we adequately clarified the clinic's policy, but sessions begin and end at specified time. If anyone is late, we still have to end on time. I'm sorry about this; I hope you don't feel slighted.
> *Mother:* No, not at all. I'm just not with it today. I mean, this is really a bad day. I almost had a wreck coming over here. I almost hit another car and had to really slam on the brakes. I thought Alex was going to go through

the windshield. I was thinking I was about to have a nervous breakdown before that. You can imagine what I'm like after that.

Therapist: [*Congruently*] I hope you don't mind my asking, but do you and Alex wear seat belts?

Mother: No.

Therapist: I wouldn't be honest if I didn't tell you that I really care about Alex and I know how much wearing a seat belt could mean to him. I would like to encourage you to strap him in when the two of you are in the car. I wish you would wear a seat belt too, not just because you're Alex's mother, but because it could be important to you as well.

Mother: I know we should use seat belts.

Therapist: I'm glad, but you say some other things are bothering you, and that makes me wonder if you would like to see someone at the clinic and talk with them about what's going on. Since I see Alex and mostly other children, I don't think that I should be that person. However, I'd be happy to arrange for someone to talk with you if you'd like.

Mother: I'm going to have to do something.

Therapist: I'll have someone call you so that you can have your own appointment when you bring Alex in next week.

The next week, Alex's mother began a psychotherapeutic relationship that lasted for two months. She reported a very volatile relationship between herself and her husband. However, she stated that things were getting better with Alex. He was less aggressive at school and was grinding his teeth less.

The relationship between Alex's father and mother was deteriorating. The mother reported a history of extramarital affairs involving both her husband and herself. Shortly after Alex entered therapy, the father announced that he planned to divorce the mother and to marry a woman who was then the wife of a military colleague.

During her fourth session, after strong encouragement from her husband, Alex's mother announced her intention to file for a divorce. She did so between the fourth and fifth session, and during the sixth session reported her intention to move to her parents' home town several hundred miles away. She said she would take Alex with her and that the father would remain where he was so as to continue with his military assignment.

Sessions six, seven, and eight with Alex were characterized by his continuing aggressive behavior and a minimum of tooth grinding. The therapist attempted to provide caring but firm limits for Alex as the boy engaged in aggressive play activities.

Sessions nine and ten with Alex were characterized by more warmth and spontaneity, less aggressive play, and minimal tooth grinding. On the eleventh session, however, Alex seemed quite subdued. The therapist had been informed that Alex knew of his parents' plans for divorce, and presumed that this was the basis for this reaction. Since he knew that Alex's mother had agreed to terminate therapy after two additional sessions, the therapist assumed that he and Alex would have a maximum of two visits following the present one.

Therapist: You seem slowed down and kind of sad today. Everything seems different. You don't even look like you'd like me to throw you up in the air.

Alex: [*To the therapist's surprise*] Throw me up in the air.

Therapist: All right. [*The therapist tosses Alex. The activity is pleasant and spontaneous, and is accompanied by laughter*] I don't think I'm going to pretend to drop you today and then catch you. There is something that I think both of us know and it's too much like dropping you to joke about.

Alex: [*Looks at therapist with puzzlement but says nothing*]

Therapist: I know your mother has talked to you about the divorce between her and your dad. I know that she's moving back to Iowa to live near your grandparents and that you're going with her. I know that I'll only see you about two times after today, and all of this makes me sad.

Alex: [*Looks at the therapist with a sad and somewhat shocked look, but says nothing*]

Therapist: I've really enjoyed being together with you. I feel like we've become good friends and enjoyed some really good times together. I feel like I've helped you too. I really believe that you're going to grow up and be a fine, healthy young man. I'll miss you.

Alex: [*Looks at the therapist briefly, then looks down and plays with some small toy cars. He says nothing, but a misty quality is apparent in his eyes*]

The final two sessions with Alex were characterized by moderate amounts of positive affect and spontaneity. The therapist eluded to termination in a matter of fact manner when it seemed appropriate. He repeated frequently that he had enjoyed his time with Alex and that he felt that Alex was growing into a happier and healthier boy. Alex remained somewhat subdued during the last two sessions. He talked very little about the play activities that he and the therapist engaged in, and he said nothing of an "in-depth" or "introspective" nature.

[*Last session, last 5 minutes*]

Therapist: Well, we're coming to the end of our last session and it's time to say good-bye. If you should ever become unhappy or have problems in the future, I hope you'll ask your mother to find someone else for you to see in Iowa. Or, if you wish, have her be in touch with me.

Alex: [*Says nothing*]

Therapist: If you ever want to write to me or send me a card, tell your mother. She has my address.

Alex: [*Does not respond either verbally or nonverbally*]

Therapist: Well, it's time for us to go. I'd like to give you a big hug. Do you feel like giving me a hug?

Alex: [*Looks hesitant at first, but walks toward the therapist*]

The therapist picked Alex up and hugged him warmly. Alex responded with a moderately enthusiastic hug. The therapist carried Alex out to the waiting room rather than walking out with him as was customary. In the waiting room they hugged again. The therapist set Alex's feet to the floor at which point he hurried from the room beckoning the mother to come quickly to the parking lot.

Therapist: [*To mother*] I would like to wish both of you the very best.

Mother: [*Nervously trying to respond to the therapist and Alex at the same time*] Thank you very much for everything you've done. We may be in touch with you if we feel like we need some help in the future. I might want Alex to talk with you on the phone, or I may need some help in locating someone for me to see in Iowa.

Therapist: Please feel free to be in touch. I'd like to help in any way I can.

Alex had already left the room and headed for the parking lot.

Alex's case illustrates some of the limited gains that can be observed in short-term psychotherapy with children and their families. Alex did show some improvements over the course of his therapy—be began to relate more approriately (less aggressively) and his tooth grinding diminished. Working with Alex also introduced his mother to the possibility of brief therapy for support during a divorce which seemed inevitable prior to Alex's entering treatment.

6

The Outcome of Therapy

As we have noted throughout this text, the goal of experiential psychotherapy is to remove barriers to the natural unfolding of the self-actualizing capability of each child. The therapist is concerned with enabling the child's own capacity for growth and healing to take the direction that is right for the child. The client's growth, creativity, fulfillment, joy, self-actualization, and individuality are encouraged. When therapy concludes, the therapist hopes that through the therapeutic relationship the child has developed and become more congruent within his or her level of growth.

Highly specific goals are avoided since they could limit the unique potentialities of each child. Children's growth can show itself in many ways. For example, children may simply feel better about themselves, or they may learn new skills and new problem-solving techniques which can be applied to other life problems. They may be happier and may experience more positive emotion. Their behavior may be more adaptive and age-appropriate, and their interpersonal relationships may become warmer and more genuine. These as well as other changes may be signs of more integrated functioning and growth.

Research on the Outcome of Therapy

The benefits of therapy are difficult to measure. Conclusive statements are hard to come by, and one finds varied claims when reviewing outcome studies. Eysenck's (1952) claims that psychotherapy is no more effective than no therapy at all served as a catalyst for much subsequent research on the outcome of psychotherapy. After making a large-scale review of outcome studies and data, Eysenck concluded that 72 percent of the clients who had received only custodial or medical care had improved, whereas only 44 percent of the clients who had received psychoanalytic treatment, and only 66 percent of the clients who had received eclectic therapy, showed improvement. Clearly, a smaller percentage of psychotherapy clients than of control clients showed improvement.

Such statistics have generated a variety of reactions. Many have questioned Eysenck's methods and conclusions. Because psychotherapy is a complex process, and because it varies for each individual, it is difficult to determine its overall effectiveness. Because of the methodological problems associated with research in this area, we are far from being able to evaluate conclusively the effectiveness of psychotherapeutic methods. Nevertheless, the debate continues.

Recent research on psychotherapy is flavored with more optimistic reports on its outcome (Bergin 1971; Frank 1979; Meltzoff and Kornreich 1970; Smith and Glass 1977). More recent reviews are also reporting that better-designed studies are more supportive of therapy than are the weaker ones (Bergin 1971; Meltzoff and Kornreich 1970). Researchers have also documented the possibility of deterioration as a result of psychotherapy. Some practices may be "psychonoxious" and may do more harm than good for the client (Bergin 1971; Hadley and Strupp 1977). Psychotherapy thus may be either beneficial or harmful. Unfortunately, we do not yet clearly understand all of the variables and interactions that determine positive or negative outcomes.

Evaluations specific to child psychotherapy show similar problems. Following Eysenck's model (1952), Levitt (1957), and Levitt, Beiser, and Robertson (1959) asserted that "there is no evidence to indicate that child psychotherapy is effective." Levitt reported that at termination of treatment two-thirds to three-fourths of the children show noticeable improvement. Follow-up studies, moreover, indicated that children maintained their improved status; at follow-up nearly 80 percent of all cases were regarded as improved. Such results sound promising for child psychotherapy until they are compared with those of the control groups. Levitt found these improvement rates to be approximately the same as those found in groups of treatment "defectors" or "terminators," that is, emotionally disturbed children who were offered formal clinic treatment but who failed to take advantage of the opportunity or institutions. Such findings may indicate the resiliency of children but not the efficacy of child psychotherapy.

Few studies of the outcome of psychotherapy with children have followed Levitt's work. Perhaps the overwhelming methodological problems inherent in such studies have inhibited efforts. Besides the usual methodologic problems associated with research, such as using adequate control groups, controlling for placebo effects, and locating former clients to follow up, research on the outcome of children's therapy also faces several additional and unique problems resulting from the clients' being children. Because the child is developing, the symptoms may change over time. Troublesome behaviors or symptoms may disappear with development, and these may be replaced by other symptoms. The child's propensity to grow out of one symptom and grow into another is not easy to deal with empirically. Also, people other than the child may be involved in therapy, and the treatment may focus on parents and parenting. When working with children and families, it is difficult to sort out and evaluate the different components of therapy. Because child therapy can be largely non-verbal, measurements of the quality of therapy that rely on verbal communication can also be misleading. Variables such as body position, eye contact, facial expression, and physical contact have an effect on the quality of the relationship and hence on the therapy itself. These important parts of therapy are difficult to assess.

While the debates about the overall effectiveness of psychotherapy continue, some professionals contend that attempts to measure the overall outcome of child psychotherapy are meaningless. An average rate of success may be impossible to determine. It seems wiser to investigate what, if anything, are the effective ingredients of therapy.

Shifting our research efforts away from general issues of outcome may ultimately help us determine whether psychotherapy for a specific individual will be helpful. We must continue to investigate the specific variables (therapist, client, technique, and situation) that are likely to affect the outcome of therapy so that we can identify the specific elements that produce positive outcomes. Rogerian psychotherapists have always been leaders in this field.

Variables that Affect the Outcome of Therapy

The Therapist

Progress in psychotherapy is related in part to the characteristics of the therapist. Rogers acknowledged early on that the qualities of the therapist are the cornerstones of therapy. We have shown throughout this text that intimacy, congruence, valuing, empathy, and responsibility are essential components in experiential psychotherapy with children.

Assessments have been made of the effect of accurate empathy, nonpossessive warmth, and congruence on the outcome of therapy with adults (see Truax and Carkhuff 1967 for a good summary, and see the 1967 report by Rogers and his colleagues concerning their experiences with severely disturbed clients in Wisconsin). The results show that the adult client's improvement correlates positively with higher levels of these three qualities in the therapist. Complementing these data are the results of Truax, Altmann, Wright, and Mitchell (1973) demonstrating the same finding with children. Their data provide some support to the general findings showing the greater therapeutic conditions of accurate empathy, nonpossessive warmth, and genuineness produce greater changes in personality and behavior. Moreover, there was some evidence from parents' evaluations to suggest a greater incidence of deterioration in children seen by therapists who provided low levels of accurate empathy, nonpossessive warmth, and genuineness. Thus child therapy may be a two-edged sword depending on the therapist's level of interpersonal skills. These three therapeutic conditions reside within the therapist; so, to a large extent, therapy is only as good as the therapist.

Other qualities of therapists have been recognized as potentially important to therapy outcome. Experienced therapists may be more effective than inexperienced ones (Strupp and Bergin 1969). In their review, Strupp and Bergin suggest that therapists' own conflicts in such areas as warmth, dependency and intimacy inhibit their clients' performance in therapy. And therapists who dislike certain clients are not likely to work well with them. The good conditions of therapy cannot be met when the therapist is not ready to relate intimately.

The Child

Progress in psychotherapy is also related to some of the characteristics of the client. Some children benefit more from therapy than do others. Some qualities of clients have been related to the outcome of therapy in traditional therapy with adults. Schofield (1964) described the ideal adult client as young, attractive, verbal, intelligent, and successful (*YAVIS* syndrome). Openness to the therapeutic process has also been viewed as a good client characteristic (Strupp and Bergin 1969). Traditional therapists have viewed the client's motivation for treatment and ability to verbalize problems and emotions as essential ingredients of successful therapy. Similarly, optimism and positive expectations about the usefulness of psychotherapy have been viewed as good signs (Wilkins 1973; Goldstein 1962a).

The client's stress may also affect the outcome of therapy. Therapists who work with adults have contended that the people who need therapy the least are the ones who receive the greatest benefit from it. Clients who begin therapy at a higher level of functioning terminate at higher levels than do those who begin at low levels (Garfield 1978). A good prognosis may be expected for a client who is experiencing distress or anxiety but whose functioning is intact. Such findings, however, have not always been supported by research. Miller and Gross (1973) contend that the relationship between improvement and the initial disturbance is curvilinear; that is, clients with little disturbance or extreme disturbance show poorer outcomes than do moderately disturbed clients.

While these and other characteristics of clients have been related to the outcome of therapy with adults, there are few parallels for psychotherapy with children. Very often, young clients are not verbal, insightful, stressed, or motivated. They may arrive in our offices with no idea of why they are there, no interest in what we are about, and no expectations for improvement. They may even have no preconception of the power and magic of the therapist. If adult clients had these characteristics, their therapists would probably suggest that they seek another source of help, but these same characteristics are fairly typical of children. Clearly, then, the characteristics of the "good" child client do not precisely match those of the "good" adult client.

While we do not yet fully understand which characteristics make some children more likely than others to benefit from therapy, we can speculate. Several qualities of young clients are emerging as relevant. Both the progress of the child's development and the clinical diagnosis seem to be important (Heinicke and Strassman 1975). Children who have different kinds of problems and diagnoses respond differently to treatment: delinquents seem to be more resistant to therapy, while children who have specific behavior disorders tend to respond better. While such patterns are emerging, it is important to use caution in interpreting such factors. Even such seemingly difficult groups as delinquents are, under certain conditions, amenable to experiential psychotherapy.

The child's developmental status may also relate to the outcome of therapy (Heinicke and Strassman 1975). Children whose development is disrupted less may show greater improvement. Such children have been less severely affected by their problems and do bring more resources to therapy. While empirical support is not yet conclusive, our experiences suggest that the child's problems and level of development do interact uniquely in ways that affect therapy and its outcome.

Therapist-Child Interactions

Therapy involves the interplay of the qualities of therapist and client, so the quality of the match between therapist and client is important to the outcome of therapy (Frank 1979; Phares 1979). Some therapists seem to work well with some clients and not as well with others.

Rogers believed that the therapist-client relationship is the cornerstone of psychotherapy. Any factors that affect the relationship may then affect the outcome of therapy. Social research and personality research suggest that similarity of attitude provides a strong basis for interpersonal attraction (Byrne 1971). Perhaps a similarity in the attitudes of therapists and clients facilitates the development of a good therapeutic relationship. Dougherty (1976) systematically matched adult clients and therapists by using a set of eleven psychological variables. He concluded that such a procedure is useful for facilitating successful therapy. Similarly, Strupp and Bergin (1969) found that the outcome is likely to be more favorable if the adult client and therapist share the same expectations about treatment. There is also evidence suggesting that adult clients do well when their level of conceptualization is similar to that of their therapist (Posthuma and Carr 1975). More study is needed to determine which combinations of traits in the therapist and the client help create good conditions for growth and change. Some of this study must be devoted to examining good and bad matches of therapists and children.

The Parents

Family characteristics are likely to be of particular importance to the outcome of psychotherapy with children (Heinicke and Strassmann 1975). Children are typically dependent on parents or other caretakers to initiate and continue their therapy, so the parents' cooperation is important. Parents may be more cooperative if they are involved in the therapy process. Studies suggest that children who remain in therapy (rather than terminate prematurely) often have both of their parents involved in that therapy (Cole and Magnussen 1967). For this and other reasons, it is important to involve both parents.

At times the child's parents are the focus of therapy. Especially when the child is very young, the therapist may work with the parents only. This unique aspect of child psychotherapy clearly shows the importance of parental involvement to the child's success.

The family's style and level of functioning may affect the outcome of the child's psychotherapy. Children from less disturbed families may show greater improvement following therapy. Cytryn, Gilbert, and Eisenberg (1960), using retrospective assessments, concluded that the parents of the children who improved most were less disturbed at the beginning of therapy and most responsive to casework. When the child's parents are experiencing problems, the child's prognosis may be linked to parental improvement: improvement in children may be closely associated with improvement in their parents (Lessing and Schilling 1966). The family's support of the child's change is also critical. Children whose families support positive change are likely to show more improvement during therapy (Kaufman et al., 1962). Thus, parents in various ways help to determine the outcome.

The Appropriateness of Experiential Psychotherapy with Children

With this book we have attempted to apply recent Rogerian thinking to work with children. The experiences of Rogers and his colleagues have provided useful insights for this work, and the continuing evolution of Rogerian theory has made therapy with children even more appropriate and useful.

We think that experiential therapy in its current form is the therapy of choice for many children who are experiencing problems. Like other ways of working with children, however, it may be more useful for some children than for others. Continuing study of the indications and contraindications for experiential therapy is needed. We do not yet have a precise empirical base to help us decide when this approach would be most useful for a specific child. However, we can begin to make some general statements as to the appropriateness of experiential psychotherapy with children. It can be helpful to many children who are experiencing emotional or behavioral problems. Throughout this text, we have attempted to show the diverse kinds of children (and their diverse problems) that can benefit from experiential therapy.

To delineate further which children can or cannot profit from experiential psychotherapy, we can note that there are development- and age-related requirements for effective intervention. To profit from direct psychotherapy, the child must have developed certain skills for relating and communicating with people. There is a general consensus that somewhere between the ages of two and four years the "typical" child client will have developed sufficiently to profit from experiential therapy. Note that the developmental requirements are not specific language requirements, since children frequently communicate and relate in other ways. Rogers (1942) noted that "between four and ten or twelve some use of play technique would almost certainly be appropriate since verbalization of significant feelings is not easy for the child at this age" (p. 74).

Just as the very young child is not an appropriate candidate for experiential therapy, so, too, would the older, severely to profoundly mentally retarded child be an inappropriate choice for this mode of therapy. But while very young or severely retarded children may not profit from direct therapy, experiential therapy may have something to offer the parents or caretakers of these children.

Other children or situations may require more than experiential psychotherapy can provide. Crisis intervention, treatment of acute medical/psychological problems, and brief consultations in primary mental health settings, for example, typically require approaches other than experiential psychotherapy. However, the good conditions of experiential therapy can enhance or facilitate these other forms of intervention. As we have noted, for some children, experiential approaches may be necessary but not sufficient. The good conditions for experiential psychotherapy are, thus, usually necessary and sometimes sufficient.

While the questions concerning the appropriate application of experiential therapy remain, we must not let the wind that rises from debate over them push us off course. Our goal is to create an atmosphere in which the child is free to use internal resources for healing. While we can help remove barriers, the strengthening of the child's inner resources is our goal. When a child's helper has learned, by a combination of instinct and training, to create the conditions that allow the child to heal and grow from within, the helper will have tapped a reservoir of internal power that can be an enormous force for good.

References

Adams, P. (1974). *A primer of child psychotherapy.* Boston: Little, Brown.

Allen, F. H. (1942). *Psychotherapy with children.* New York: Norton.

American Academy of Pediatrics, Task Force on Pediatric Education. (1978). *The future of pediatric education.* Washington, D.C.: American Academy of Pediatrics.

Arnold, L. E. (1978). Strategies and tactics of parent guidance. In L. E. Arnold (Ed.), *Helping Parents Help Their Children.* New York: Brunner/Mazel.

Axline, V. M. (1947). *Play therapy.* Boston: Houghton Mifflin.

Axline, V. M. (1964). *Dibs: In search of self.* Boston: Houghton Mifflin.

Bandura, A. (1969). *Principles of behavior modification.* New York: Holt, Rinehart and Winston.

Baruch, D. W. (1949). *New ways in discipline.* New York: McGraw-Hill.

Bergin, A. E. (1971). The evaluation of therapeutic outcomes. In A. E. Bergin & S. L. Garfield (Eds.), *Handbook of psychotherapy and behavior change.* New York: Wiley.

Berkowitz, B. P., & Graziano, A. M. (1972). Training parents as behavior therapists: A review. *Behavior Research and Therapy, 10,* 297–317.

Bonner, B., & Everett, F. (1982). Influence of client preparation and therapist prognostic expectations on children's attitudes and expectations of psychotherapy. *Journal of Clinical Child Psychology, 11,* 202–8.

Bonner, B., & Everett, F. (in press). Influence of client preparation and problem severity on attitudes and expectations in child psychotherapy. *Professional Psychology: Research and Practice.*

Bourne, L. (1974, April). "Applications of Contemporary Cognitive Psychology." Address presented at the meeting of the Southwestern Psychological Association, Oklahoma City.

Byrne, D. (1971). *The attraction paradigm.* New York: Holt, Rinehart, and Winston.

Caplan, G. (1964). *Principles of preventive psychiatry.* New York: Basic Books.

Carkhuff, R. R., & Bierman, R. (1970). Training as a mode of treatment of parents of emotionally disturbed children. *Journal of Counseling Psychology, 17,* 157–61.

Clarizio, H. F., & McCoy, G. F. (1976). *Behavioral disorders in children.* New York: Crowell.

Cole, J. K., & Magnussen, M. G. (1967). Family situation factors related to remainers and terminators of treatment. *Psychotherapy, 4,* 107–9.

Cooper, S., & Wanerman, L. (1977). *Children in treatment.* New York: Brunner/Mazel.

Cytryn, L., Gilbert, A., & Eisenberg, L. (1960). The effectiveness of tranquilizing drugs plus supportive psychotherapy in treating behavior disorders of children. *American Journal of Orthopsychiatry, 30,* 113–28.

Day, L., & Reznikoff, M. (1980). Preparation of children and parents for treatment at a children's psychiatric clinic through videotaped modeling. *Journal of Consulting and Clinical Psychology, 48*(2), 303–4.

Dollard, J., & Miller, N. (1950). *Personality and psychotherapy: An analysis in terms of learning, thinking, and culture.* New York: McGraw-Hill.

Dorfman, E. (1951). Play therapy. In C. Rogers (Ed.), *Client-centered therapy.* Boston: Houghton Mifflin.

Dougherty, F. E. (1976). Patient-therapist matching for prediction of optimal and minimal outcome. *Journal of Consulting and Clinical Psychology, 44,* 889–97.

Duff, R. S., Rowe, D. S., & Anderson, F. P. (1972). Patient care and student learning in a pediatric clinic. *Pediatrics, 50,* 839–46.

Erickson, M. T. (1978). *Child psychopathology: Assessment, etiology, and treatment.* Englewood Cliffs, NJ: Prentice-Hall.

Everett, F. (1983). Parent dilemma: When is a problem a problem? *Perspectives, 11*(2), 1, 7.

Eysenck, H. J. (1952). The effects of psychotherapy: An evaluation. *Journal of Consulting Psychology, 16,* 319–24.

Farley, O., Peterson, K., & Spanos, G. (1975). Self termination from a child guidance center. *Community Mental Health Journal, 11,* 325–34.

Festinger, L. (1957). *Theory of cognitive dissonance.* Evanston, IL: Row, Peterson and Co.

Fiedler, F. E. (1950). A comparison of therapeutic relationships in psychoanalytic, nondirective and Adlerian therapy. *Journal of Consulting Psychology, 14,* 436–45.

Frank, J. D. (1959). The dynamics of the psychotherapeutic relationship: Determinants and effects of the therapist's influence. *Psychiatry, 22,* 17–39.

Frank, J. D. (1971). Therapeutic factors in psychotherapy. *American Journal of Psychotherapy, 25,* 350–61.

Frank, J. D. (1973). Persuasion and healing. *A comparative study of psychotherapy* (Rev. ed.). Baltimore: Johns Hopkins University Press.

Frank, J. D. (1979). The present status of outcome studies. *Journal of Consulting and Clinical Psychology, 47,* 310–16.

Freud, A. (1946). *The psychoanalytic treatment of children* (1926). New York: International Universities Press.

Freud, A. (1965). *Normality and pathology in childhood: Assessments of development.* New York: International Universities Press.

Freud, S. (1959). Analysis of a phobia in a five-year-old boy. In *Collected papers* (J. Riviere, Trans.). New York: Basic Books.

Fuchs, N. R. (1957). Play therapy at home. *The Merrill-Palmer Quarterly, 3,* 89–95.

Garfield, S. L. (1978). Research on client variables in psychotherapy. In S. L. Garfied & A. E. Bergin (Eds.), *Handbook of psychotherapy and behavior change* (2nd ed.). New York: Wiley.

Gendlin, E. T. (1974). A short summary and some long predictions. In D. A. Wexler & L. N. Rice (Eds.), *Client-centered and experiential psychotherapy.* New York: Wiley.

Gendlin, E. T. (1981). *Focusing.* New York: Bantam Books.

Gendlin, E. T. (1986). *Let your body interpret your dreams.* Wilmette, IL: Chiron.

Glidewell, J., & Swallow, C. (1968). *The prevalence of maladjustment in elementary schools.* Chicago: University of Chicago Press.

Golden, B. (1969, September). *Conceptual and methodological problems in monitored play therapy.* Paper presented at the meeting of the American Psychological Association, Washington, D.C.

Goldstein, A. P. (1962a). Participant expectancies in psychotherapy. *Psychiatry, 25,* 72–79.

Goldstein, A. P. (1962b). *Therapist-patient expectancies in psychotherapy.* New York: Macmillan.

Goldstein, A. P. (1966). Prognostic and role expectancies in psychotherapy. *American Journal of Psychotherapy, 20,* 35–44.

Gordon, T. (1971). *Parent effectiveness training.* New York: Wyden Books.

Gordon, T. (speaker). (1976). *Parent effectiveness* [KPBS Education TV]. San Diego, CA.

Guerney, B. G. (1964). Filial therapy: Description and rationale. *Journal of Consulting Psychology, 28,* 304–10.

Guerney, L. (1976). Play therapy: A training manual for parents. In C. Schaefer, *The therapeutic use of child's play.* New York: Jason Aronson.

Hadley, S. W., & Strupp, H. H. (1977). Evaluations of treatment in psychotherapy: Naivete or necessity? *Professional Psychology, 8,* 478–90.

Hart, J. (1974). Beyond psychotherapy—The applied psychology of the future. In D. A. Wexler & L. N. Rice (Eds.), *Innovations in client-centered therapy.* New York: Wiley.

Heinicke, C. M., & Strassmann, L. H. (1975). Toward more effective research on child psychotherapy. *American Academy of Child Psychiatry, 14,* 561–88.

Hereford, C. (1963). *Changing parental attitudes through group discussion.* Austin: University of Texas Press.

Hobbs, N. (1962). Sources of gain in psychotherapy. *American Psychologist, 17,* 741–47.

Holmes, D., & Urie, R. (1975). Effects of preparing children for psychotherapy. *Journal of Consulting and Clinical Psychology, 43,* 311–18.

Horney, K. (1939). *New ways in psychoanalysis.* New York: Norton.

Johnson, C. A., & Katz, R. C. (1973). Using parents as change agents for their children: A review. *Journal of Child Psychology and Psychiatry, 14,* 181–200.

Joint Commission on Mental Health of Children. (1970). *Crisis in child mental health: Challenge for the 1970's.* New York: Harper & Row.

Kaufman, I., Frank, T., Friend, J., Heims, L. W., & Weiss, R. (1962). Success and failure in the treatment of childhood schizophrenia. *American Journal of Psychiatry, 118,* 909–13.

Klein, M. (1932). *The psychoanalysis of children.* London: Hogarth.

Lapouse, R., & Monk, M. (1958). An epidemiologic study of behavior characteristics in children. *American Journal of Public Health, 48,* 1134–44.

Lapouse, R., & Monk, M. (1964). Behavior deviations in a representative sample of children. *American Journal of Orthopsychiatry, 34,* 436–46.

Lessing, E. E., & Schilling, F. H. (1966). Relationship between treatment selection variables and treatment outcome in a child guidance clinic. *American Academy of Child Psychiatry, 5*, 313–48.

Levitt, E. E. (1957). The results of psychotherapy with children: An evaluation. *Journal of Consulting Psychology, 21*, 189–96.

Levitt, E. E. (1958). Parents' reasons for defection from treatment at a child guidance clinic. *Mental Hygiene, 42*, 521–24.

Levitt, E. E. (1971). Research on psychotherapy with children. In A. E. Bergin & S. L. Garfield (Eds.), *Handbook of psychotherapy and behavior change*. New York: Wiley.

Levitt, E. E., Beiser, H. R., & Robertson, R. E. (1959). A follow-up evaluation of cases treated at a community child guidance clinic. *American Journal of Orthopsychiatry, 29*, 337–47.

MacFarlane, J., Allen, L., & Honzik, M. (1954). *A developmental study of the behavior problems of normal children between twenty-one months and fourteen years*. Berkeley: University of California Press.

Meltzoff, J., & Kornreich, M. (1970). *Research on psychotherapy*. New York: Atherton.

Miller, J. O., & Gross, S. J. (1973). Curvilinear trends in outcome research. *Journal of Consulting Psychology, 41*, 242–44.

Mira, M. (1970). Results of a behavior modification training program for parents and teachers. *Behavior Research and Therapy, 8*, 309–11.

Moustakas, C. W. (1965). *Existential child therapy, the child's discovery of himself*. New York: Basic Books.

Moustakas, C. W. (1959). *Psychotherapy with children*. New York: Harper & Row.

Patterson, C. H. (1958). The place of values in counseling and psychotherapy. *Journal of Counseling Psychology, 5*(3), 216–23.

Phares, E. J. (1979). *Clinical psychology: Concepts, methods, and profession*. Homewood, IL: Dorsey Press.

Piaget, J. (1969). *Psychology of the child*. New York: Basic Books.

Piaget, J. (1983). Piaget's theory. In P. Mussen (Ed.), *Handbook of Child Psychology* (Vol. I., 4th. ed.). New York: Wiley.

Porter, E. H. (1950). *Therapeutic counseling*. Boston: Houghton Mifflin.

Posthuma, A. B., & Carr, J. E. (1975). Differentiation matching in psychotherapy. *Canadian Psychological Review, 16*, 35–43.

President's Commission on Mental Health. (1978). *Report of the task panel on mental health and American families: Sub-task panel on infants, children, and adolescents*.

Raskin, N. J. (1950). Developments in client-centered therapy. In L. E. Abt & D. Brower (Eds.), *Progress in clinical psychology*. (Vol. I). New York: Grune & Stratton.

Raskin, N. J. (1951). The nondirective attitude. In C. R. Rogers, Client-centered therapy (p. 29). Boston: Houghton Mifflin. (Original work written 1947, unpublished).

Richardson, D., & Cohen, R. (1968). A follow-up study of a sample of child psychiatry dropouts. *Mental Hygiene, 52*, 535–41.

Robinson, F. (1950). Are nondirective techniques sometimes too directive? *Readings in Modern Methods of Counseling*. New York: Appleton-Century-Crofts.

Rogers, C. R. (1942). *Counseling and psychotherapy*. Boston: Houghton Mifflin.

Rogers, C. R. (1951). *Client-centered therapy*. Boston: Houghton Mifflin.

Rogers, C. R. (1957). The necessary and sufficient conditions of therapeutic personality change. *Journal of Consulting Psychology, 21,* 95–103.

Rogers, C. R. (1962). Some learnings from a study of psychotherapy with schizophrenics. *Pennsylvania Psychiatric Quarterly (Summer),* 3–15.

Rogers, C. R. (1969). *Freedom to learn.* Columbus, OH: Merrill.

Rogers, C. R. (1973). Some new challenges. *American Psychologist, 28,* 379–87.

Rogers, C. R. (1975a). An unappreciated way of being. *The Counseling Psychologist, 5,* 2–9.

Rogers, C. R. (1975b). Client-centered psychotherapy. In A. M. Friedman, H. I. Kaplan, & B. J. Sadock (Eds.), *Comprehensive textbook of psychiatry.* Baltimore: Williams & Wilkins.

Rogers, C. R. (1977). *Carl Rogers on Personal Power.* New York: Dell (Delacorte Press).

Rogers, C. R., Gendlin, E. T., Kiesler, D. J., & Truax, C. B. (1967). *The therapeutic relationship and its impact: A study of psychotherapy with schizophrenics.* Madison, WI: University of Wisconsin Press.

Rutter, M. (1975). *Helping troubled children.* New York: Plenum.

Schofield, W. (1964). *Psychotherapy: The purchase of friendship.* Englewood Cliffs, NJ: Prentice-Hall.

Seeman, J. (1965). Perspectives in client-centered therapy. In B. J. Wolman (Ed.), *Handbook of clinical psychology.* New York: McGraw-Hill.

Smith, M. L., & Glass, G. V. (1977). Meta-analysis of psychotherapy outcome studies. *American Psychologist, 32,* 752–60.

Stover, L., & Guerney, B. G. (1967). The efficacy of training procedures for mothers in filial therapy. *Psychotherapy: Theory, Research and Practice, 4,* 110–15.

Strupp, H. H. (1973). *Psychotherapy: Clinical, research and theoretical issues.* New York: Jason Aronson.

Strupp, H. H., & Bergin, A. E. (1969). Some empirical and conceptual bases for coordinated research in psychotherapy: A critical review of issues, trends, and evidence. *International Journal of Psychiatry, 7,* 18–90.

Sullivan, H. S. (1947). *Conceptions of modern psychiatry.* Washington, D.C.: William Alanson White Psychiatric Foundation.

Sullivan, H. S. (1953). *The interpersonal theory of psychiatry.* New York: Norton.

Tharp, R. G., & Wetzel, R. (1969). *Behavior modification in the natural environment.* New York: Academic Press.

Truax, C. B. (1961). Process of group therapy: Relationships between hypothesized therapeutic conditions and intrapersonal exploration. *Psychological Monographs, 75(7),* 1–35.

Truax, C. B. (1966). Effective ingredients of psychotherapy: An approach to unraveling the patient-therapist interaction. In G. E. Stollack, B. G. Guerney, Jr., & M. Rothberg (Eds.), *Psychotherapy research: Selected readings.* Chicago: Rand McNally.

Truax, C. B., Altmann, H., Wright, L., & Mitchell, K. M. (1973). Effects of therapeutic conditions in child therapy. *Journal of Community Psychology, 1,* 313–18.

Truax, C. B., & Carkhuff, R. R. (1964). Significant development in psychotherapy research. In L. E. Abt & B. F. Riess (Eds.), *Progress in Clinical Psychology* (Vol. 6). New York: Grune & Stratton.

Truax, C. B., & Carkhuff, R. R. (1965). Experimental manipulations of therapeutic conditions. *Journal of Consulting Psychology, 29,* 119–24.

Truax, C. B., & Carkhuff, R. R. (1967). *Toward effective counseling and psychotherapy: Training and practice.* Chicago: Aldine.

Truax, C. B., & Mitcheil, K. M. (1968). The psychotherapeutic and the psychonoxious: Human encounters that change behavior. In M. J. Feldman (Ed.), *Studies in psychotherapy and behavioral change.* New York: State University of New York at Buffalo.

Weiss, S., & Dlugokinski, E. (1974). Parental expectations of psychotherapy. *The Journal of Psychology, 86,* 71–80.

Werry, J., & Quay, H. (1971). The prevalence of behavior symptoms in younger elementary school children. *American Journal of Orthopsychiatry, 41,* 136–43.

Wilkins, W. (1973). Expectancy of therapeutic gain: An empirical and conceptual critique. *Journal of Consulting and Clinical Psychology, 40,* 69–77.

Wolpe, J. (1969). *The practice of behavior therapy.* Elmsford, N.Y.: Pergamon Press.

Woods, T. A. (1978). A comparison of mothers' expectations and child psychotherapists' expectations of child psychotherapy (Doctoral dissertation, Northwestern University, 1977). *Dissertation Abstracts International, 38*(5), 4494–95B.

Wright, L. (1970). *Techniques in child rearing* [Oklahoma Educational Television Authority (series)]. Norman, OK.

Wright, L. (1976). Indirect treatment of children through principle-oriented parent consultation. *Journal of Counseling and Clinical Psychology, 44,* 148.

Wright, L. (1978). Group consultation and bibliotherapeutic aids. *Feelings and Their Medical Significance, 20*(5), 21–24.

Wright, L. (1982). Primary versus secondary and tertiary levels of mental health care. *Clinical Psychologist, 35,* 3–4.

Wright, L. (in press). Psychology and pediatrics: Prospects for cooperative efforts to promote child health. *American Psychologist.*

Wright, L., Schaefer, A., & Solomons, G. (1979). *Encyclopedia of pediatric psychology.* Baltimore: University Park Press.

Zaro, J., Barach, R., Nedelman, D., & Dreivlatt, I. (1977). *A guide for beginning psychotherapists.* Cambridge: Cambridge University Press.

Zigler, E. F. (1974). Children's needs in the seventies: A federal perspective. In G. J. Williams & S. Gordan (Eds.), *Clinical child psychology: Current practices and future perspectives.* New York: Behavioral Publications.

Index

Logan Wright is clinical professor of psychology at the Oklahoma University Health Sciences Center and head of the Wright Foundation and Institute of Health Psychology for Children in Oklahoma City, Oklahoma. He is the author of several books, including *Parent Power,* and is the 1986 president of the American Psychological Association.

Frances Everett is director of the Psychology Division of the Guidance Service of the Oklahoma State Department of Health. She is the author of numerous articles in the area of child clinical psychology.

Lois Roisman is executive director of the Jewish Fund for Justice in Washington, D.C. She worked on this book while she was Director of Editorial Services at the Oklahoma University Health Sciences Center.